Star Chart for the Northern Skies

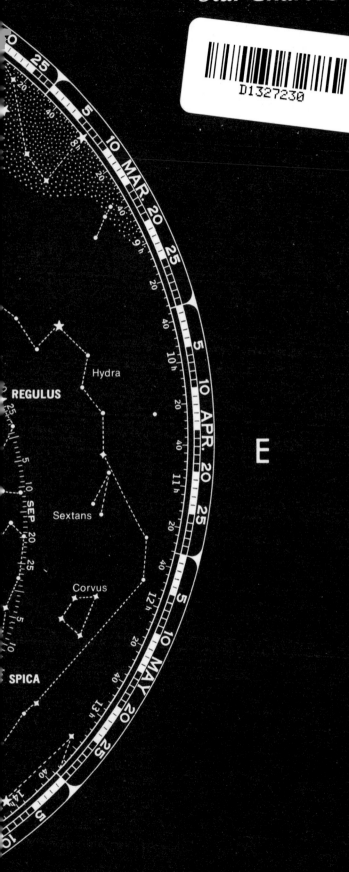

E

THE CONSTELLATIONS

Aquarius –The Water Carrier
Aquila –The Eagle
Auriga –The Charioteer
Boötes –The Bear Driver (The Herdsman)
Cancer –The Crab
Canis Major –The Larger Dog
Canis Minor –The Smaller Dog
Capricornus –The Sea Goat
Cassiopeia –The Royal Queen
Cepheus –The Queen's Royal Consort
Cetus –The Whale
Columba –The Dove
Corona Borealis –The Northern Crown
Corvus –The Crow
Cygnus –The Swan (The Northern Cross)
Delphinus –The Dolphin
Draco –The Dragon
Eridanus –The River
Gemini –The Twins
Hercules –The Hero
Hydra –The Sea Serpent
Leo –The Lion
Lepus –The Hare
Libra –The Scale (The Claws of the Scorpion)
Lyra –The Lyre
Ophiuchus –The Serpent Bearer
Orion –The Hunter
Pegasus –The Flying Horse
Perseus –The Slayer of Medusa
Pisces –The Fish
Piscis Austrinus –The Southern Fish
Pleiades –The Seven Sisters
Sagittarius –The Archer
Serpens Caput –The Serpent's Head
Serpens Cauda –The Serpent's Tail
Sextans –The Sextant
Scorpius –The Scorpion
Taurus –The Bull
Triangulum –The Triangle
Ursa Major –The Great Bear (The Big Dipper)
Ursa Minor –The Little Bear (The Little Dipper)
Virgo –The Virgin

Album of
Astronomy

By TOM McGOWEN

Illustrated by ROD RUTH

RAND McNALLY & COMPANY
Chicago · New York · San Francisco

Text and illustrations reviewed and authenticated by
James A. Seevers, B.S., Astronomer
Larry A. Ciupik, M.S., Astronomer

Library of Congress Cataloging in Publication Data
McGowen, Tom.
  Album of astronomy.
  SUMMARY: An introduction to astronomy including
a survey of the solar system, stars, comets, and the universe.
  1. Astronomy—Juvenile literature.
[1. Astronomy] I. Ruth, Rod. II. Title.
QB46.M2   520   79-9485
ISBN 0-528-82048-6
ISBN 0-528-80048-5 lib. bdg.

First printing, 1979

Contents

The Universe—GLITTERING BLACKNESS

ON A CLEAR NIGHT, in some open place where there are no city lights nearby to throw their glare into the sky, you can look up and see a vast, deep blackness glittering with what seems like thousands of tiny points of light. You are looking through the atmosphere, Earth's blanket of air, into a portion of the universe.

What *is* that enormous darkness in which the stars glitter? We call it space, and it is literally emptiness and nothingness. It is an airless, waterless *void*. And it is endless. It goes on forever! Think about that for a while, and you'll get dizzy!

But although space itself is emptiness, there are many things within it. Stars, such as our hot, glowing sun. Planets, such as Earth. Moons. Comets. Chunks of rock called asteroids and meteoroids. Tiny bits of gas and gigantic clouds of dust and gas.

And space is also filled with what scientists call energy or radiation—streams of light, heat, and radio waves, x-rays, gamma rays, ultraviolet rays, microwaves, and cosmic rays (tiny, tiny particles). So, you might say space is the emptiness surrounding all the various things *in* space.

Space and all the things in it make up what we call the universe. The parts of the universe we can see from the earth, with just our eyes, are space, the stars, and a few planets. Only about 5,000 stars can be seen at night from either part of the earth, above or below the equator. But with the largest telescopes, *billions* of stars can be seen. Does that sound like a lot? Actually, what we see is only a tiny fraction of all the stars in the universe!

You see, stars are gathered together in huge groups called galaxies. In the galaxy

to which our star, the sun, belongs, there are more than 150 billion stars. And there are probably billions of other galaxies besides the one we are in; some with millions of stars and some with more than a trillion. All in all, scientists think there may be more than *200 billion billion* stars in the universe—a number so great our minds can barely understand it!

The distances between stars in a galaxy are enormous, and the distances between galaxies are even more enormous. The closest star to our sun is the star named Proxima Centauri. It is about 25 million million—that's 25 *trillion*—miles away from Earth. Yet this star and our sun are in the same galaxy. And there are other stars in this galaxy thousands of times farther away than Proxima Centauri.

birth of a star
(Orion Nebula)

Actually, most distances in space are so vast that scientists don't measure them in miles. Space distances are measured in what are called light-years. Light is the fastest moving thing in the universe. It travels at a speed of 186,282 miles a second. Thus, light can move 5.88 trillion miles in a year, so a light-year equals 5.88 trillion miles. Proxima Centauri, 25 trillion miles away, is about 4.3 light-years away. But there are stars in our own galaxy, the Milky Way, which are as much as 80,000 light-years away, while the galaxies farthest from ours are billions of light-years away. As you can see, distances in the universe are so great, and the farthest distances are so uncertain, that the size of the universe is not definitely known.

As a matter of fact, the universe may not even *have* a certain size. For the galaxies aren't just "hanging" in space, they are moving. Most galaxies are grouped in clusters, and these clusters are moving away from each other in all directions. The universe is *expanding,* like an inflating balloon.

To understand how and why this is happening, you have to understand how most astronomers think the universe began. They think it began with the "Big Bang"—literally an enormous explosion!

According to the Big Bang theory, at one time all matter (or material now present in the universe that makes up stars, planets, clouds of gas, and everything else) was tightly squeezed into a single, gigantic, superhot "blob." Some time between 10 and 20 billion years ago, this "cosmic fireball," as it is sometimes called, exploded.

At that moment, what we know as space, time, and the universe were created. Fragments of glowing matter were hurled out in all directions, forming the first stars and galaxies. And the galaxy clusters are still moving through space in the same directions in which they started out. So the universe is continuing to expand. If you want to see how this is happening, paint a sprinkling of dots on a balloon, then slowly blow up the balloon. You can see the dots spread apart from one another in all directions, just as the universe's galaxy groups are gradually doing.

Some astronomers think the universe will continue to expand *forever*. But they also think that gravity, the mysterious force that pulls all things in space toward one another, will slowly pull the galaxies in each cluster of galaxies together until a number of enormous "supergalaxies" are formed. Then, gravity will slowly draw all the stars in each supergalaxy together into single, huge masses—and these great, redly glowing masses will drift on forever into the unending black emptiness, growing ever farther and farther apart, until they are all separated from one another by unimaginable, endless distances. And thus, the universe as we know it would end!

But other astronomers have a different idea. They think that, at some time in the far future, the universe will stop expanding. They believe the galaxies will begin to lose speed and will start to "fall back." As the galaxies begin to come closer together, gravity will slowly draw each of them into a single, tight mass. In this manner, all the

6

matter in the universe will once again come together! And when all the matter in the universe is together, as it was before the Big Bang, there would be *another* Big Bang, and a new universe would be formed. In fact, according to this theory, this is probably how our universe first came to be— from the collapse of a previous universe!

A small group of astronomers has still another idea about the universe. They think it will continue to expand, but they also think new matter is constantly being created and new galaxies are constantly being born. Thus, for these scientists, the universe will never end. And it never *began*. They think that it has always existed and will always exist, forever.

All of these questions about the beginning and end of the universe are really a long way from being answered. Scientists need to learn a great deal more about the way the universe works before they can say for sure how it began, how it will end, or whether it has existed forever.

A question that comes into the mind of almost anyone who looks up at the twinkling stars in space, is: Are there other intelligent living beings out there, somewhere, or are we all alone in the universe?

Astronomers are in almost complete agreement on the answer to that question. They feel that life is probably quite *common* throughout the universe!

In the first place, life can only come into being on a certain kind of planet, and from what we know about the way stars are "born," it seems clear that families of

planets, like the family of planets that belongs to our sun, are often born along with certain kinds of stars. Of the 10 or 12 stars closest to our sun, some evidence suggests that about half may have smaller objects near them, objects that appear to be planets about the size of our solar system's biggest planet, Jupiter. Thus, some of those stars may also have small planets, like our sun has, planets that we just can't detect yet. Some astronomers feel that in our galaxy alone there could be billions of planets, similar to Earth, that could have living things on them. And it is the guess of many astronomers that, of all those planets that could have life, there might be as many as a million where there may be intelligent creatures that could have a civilization like ours. And remember, this is only in *our* galaxy—not even counting all the other billions of galaxies!

So, as you look up at the stars in the night sky, remember you are seeing only a tiny, tiny few of all the stars there are—in fact, only a tiny, tiny few of all the stars in our galaxy alone. Remember that most stars in the universe are so far away, the twinkling light from them may have been traveling for hundreds, thousands, or even millions of years before it reached your eyes. And remember that some of those stars may have planets like Earth. And, on some of those planets, perhaps at the very instant you are looking at the glittering universe, an intelligent creature may be looking at the sky and thinking: I wonder if there's life out there!

The Sun—STAR WITH A FAMILY

ITS SURFACE is a titanic, rippling, writhing ocean of flame, from which gigantic spurts of white-hot, glowing gas curve upward for thousands of miles, then fall back. Its center is literally an enormous, continuously exploding hydrogen bomb, turning out incredible amounts of energy every second and sending it up to the surface and out into space to hurtle through the darkness as waves of heat and light. It is an awesome, incredible, roaring, radiating giant! It is a star—Earth's star, the sun.

The sun, like all stars, is a gigantic ball of gas. Now gas as we think of it is thin and "airy" stuff, but in the sun it is squeezed together so tightly by gravity that most of it is as thick as water, and it is as thick as mud near the center. The very center is probably thicker and harder than the thickest, hardest rock on Earth! When matter is squeezed together this tightly it becomes incredibly hot. *Thermonuclear energy,* the energy created when hydrogen atoms combine to form helium in a process called atomic fusion, rages at the sun's center. The surface glows with a tremendously high temperature. The sun, a huge sphere, glows just as a piece of white-hot steel glows when it comes out of the furnace of a steel mill.

But the sun glows with such brilliance that we can't look directly at it from even 93 million miles away, standing on the surface of Earth. For the sun is many, many times hotter, and therefore brighter, than a piece of white-hot steel. The temperature of its surface is some 10 thousand degrees, and the temperature of its center, where the energy is produced, is about 27 *million* degrees!

Compared to Earth, the sun is immense. It is about 865 thousand miles wide. If the sun were the size of a ball about six inches wide, Earth would be the size of a pinhead beside it. Yet, as stars go, the sun is not really very big at all. Many stars are much larger.

When you glance at the sun for a moment, you get the impression that its face is smooth and clear. But in actuality the sun's surface is torn by intensely violent "storms." Curves and loops of glowing gas, called prominences, often rise up from the surface like a spectacular fireworks display. A prominence may stretch as wide as 120 thousand miles and shoot up to a height of 20 thousand miles. It may suddenly explode, hurling masses of gas and energy into space. Prominences are caused by

8

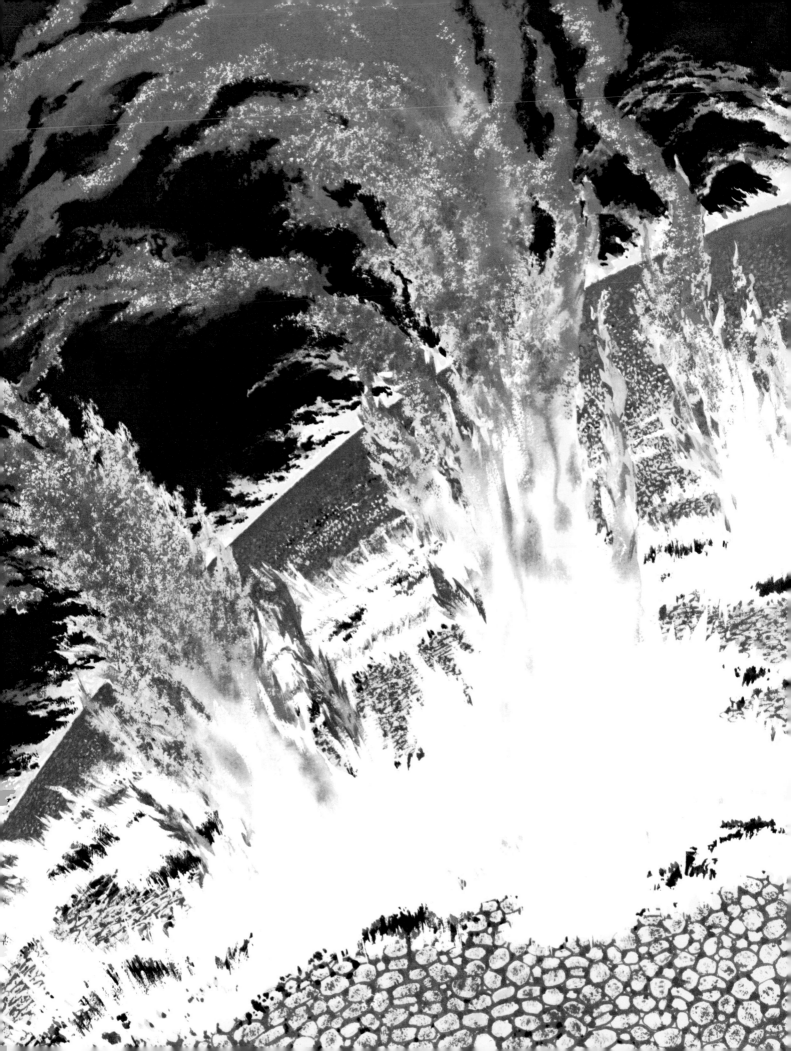

magnetic forces at work within the sun.

At certain times, dark spots known as sunspots appear on the sun's face. Like prominences, they are caused by magnetic forces. In fact, a sunspot itself is actually a gigantic magnet of tremendous power. An ordinary-sized sunspot is big enough to swallow up the whole planet Earth. These spots appear darker than the rest of the sun's surface because they are much less hot and therefore much less bright. They are less hot because their strong magnetism blocks off the flow of hot gases from inside the sun.

Depending on their size, sunspots last for several days to several weeks or even months, slowly breaking up into clusters that generally fade away. At times, however, a tremendous explosion called a solar flare may occur near a group of sunspots. It may last from a few minutes to an hour.

The sun has a "family" of planets and other objects that circle around it at various distances, and the sun and everything that circles it is known as the solar system. (The word *solar* comes from the sun's name, Sol, which is the name of an ancient sun god.) The planets are all far, far smaller than the sun, and they do not glow with their own light as the sun does. Some of the twinkling lights we see in the sky at night are planets, but they are not twinkling with their own light—they are shining with *reflected* sunlight.

The planets move around the sun in oval paths; the oval shape is called an ellipse. The path of a planet around the sun (or of any object in space around any other object) is called an orbit. The length of time that it takes a planet to orbit the sun once is the planet's year. As each planet moves around the sun, it is also rotating, or spinning slowly, like a top. The length of time it takes a planet to make one full spin, or rotation in space, can be called the planet's day.

Why do the planets move in orbit around the sun instead of just moving through space in straight lines? It is because of the pull of the mysterious force we call gravity. Larger objects in space tend to pull smaller ones toward them. You see, each planet is "trying" to move in a straight line, but the pull of the sun's gravity won't let it. If you tie a tennis ball to a long string, you can swing the ball in a circle, like a planet moving around the sun. Let go of the string and the ball will fly away, but as long as you hold the string, the ball can only go around and around your hand. The string is like the pull of gravity that keeps each planet in orbit.

The sun, too, is moving, as all things in space are. It rotates at the rate of about one full turn an Earth-month. And it is also moving in an enormous orbit around the center of our galaxy, carrying its system of circling objects with it. It takes the sun about 200 million Earth-years to make one complete trip around the center of the galaxy. This trip is sometimes called the cosmic year.

Where did this star and its family come from? Were they formed during the Big Bang? The answer is no, since the Big Bang occurred more than 16 billion years ago,

and the sun is only about 5 billion years old. Scientists think the sun did begin with an explosion—the explosion of a huge, old star somewhere in space billions of years ago.

That ancient explosion threw off an enormous cloud of dust and gas. The cloud contained many kinds of light and heavy chemical elements, which are the materials from which all things are formed. But for the most part, the cloud was made up of hydrogen gas.

The cloud drifted through space and mixed with other clouds. Many such clouds can be seen drifting in space today. Gravity slowly pulled the new cloud mixture together, finally forming a single, huge mass of gas and dust. As the cloud pulled together, it began rotating. And it flattened into a huge disk shape.

The steady pull of gravity tugged much of the gas in toward the center of the mass, where it began to take shape. Because the gas was being pulled into it equally from all directions, the mass took the shape of a ball. As it grew ever larger, its gravity grew stronger, and it pulled more matter into itself. It became an enormous globe made up mostly of hydrogen gas. Gravity pulled it ever tighter, especially at the center where it had first begun to form. Under this tremendous pressure, the center of the globe grew hotter and hotter. It began to glow ever brighter as it heated up. At its center, it began to change the gas of which it was made into energy—heat, light, and radiation. And thus the sun was born.

As this was happening, gravity was also at work in the farther-out parts of the great gassy disk. Bits of dust and gas were drawn together, forming clumps. As the clumps grew bigger, their gravity pulled harder, bringing still more gas and dust into them. Like the sun, they became tight-packed balls of matter, only far smaller, and in most cases, far more solid than the sun. They, too, grew hot from being squeezed together, but they did not have enough matter to become stars. And thus the solar system was formed—nine planet-balls, some of them accompanied by smaller moon-balls, together with lumps of rock and ice mixed with rock, all revolving around the huge, central sun-ball, just as the gassy disk had originally revolved around its center.

And will this great, glowing ball at the center of the solar system ever *stop* glowing? Yes, it will. But because of its huge size and the enormous amount of gas it contains, this will not happen for about another 5 billion years. When it does begin to happen, the sun will first swell up, becoming red in color and so large it will swallow the inner planets—including Earth! It will then slowly shrink down until it is no bigger than Earth, and for some billions of years it will glow with a hot, white light. Slowly, then, the sun's light will fade as the last of its energy is used up, and finally our star will become a shrunken, dark, burned-out cinder, moving silently through space, surrounded by dead, cold planets.

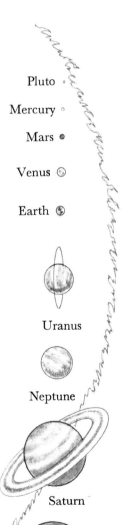

section of the sun's surface and the size of the planets

Pluto

Mercury

Mars

Venus

Earth

Uranus

Neptune

Saturn

Jupiter

Mercury —SWIFT TRAVELER

YOU ARE STANDING on a bleak, rocky plain dotted as far as your eyes can see with round pits of various sizes. In the distance rises a long line of steep cliffs. The sky is pitch black and filled with bright, unwinking stars.

All at once there is a glare upon the horizon. The sun is rising. But *what* a sun! It is a huge, blazing ball, more than twice as big as the sun you see in Earth's sky. And, as the sun rises, the sky does not slowly turn bright and blue as it would on Earth—it stays night-black and filled with stars.

Very slowly the big, glowing disk moves upward until all of it can be seen perched on the horizon. On Earth, the sun would continue climbing into the sky. But here something different happens. The sun begins to set again! Slowly, it drops back below the horizon—and is gone for what would be several Earth-days. Is that all the higher the sun ever gets in this place?

But, wait a bit—here it comes again! It's rising for a *second* time! And this time it moves on up into the sky, which still stays black as night. And, as the sun rises higher, until it is nearly overhead, it gets smaller— as if somehow it was getting farther away!

But then, as it begins to drop back down toward the horizon, it gradually gets bigger. By the time it is ready to set, it has once more become enormous!

Now, all this hasn't happened in just 24 hours or so, as it does on Earth. It has taken this sun an amount of time equal to 88 Earth-days (or 88 24-hour cycles) to move across the sky!

As you watch, the big sun slowly sets. But, once again, something strange happens. For, after the sun seems to have set, it comes rising up over the horizon again, pauses there for a bit, and then sets once more, for the *third* time this day! And now you won't see it again for a time equal to 88 Earth-days.

This strange place you have just visited in imagination is a spot on what's called the terminator (a planet's "edge" between its sunlit and dark sides) of the planet Mercury, at the time when the planet is nearest to the sun in its orbit. Mercury is the closest to the sun of all the planets, only 36 million miles away (Earth, at 93 million miles, is almost three times farther away). This, of course, is why the sun would look so much bigger than it does from Earth. And because Mercury is so close to the sun,

12

terminator
(line between light and dark)

its year—the length of time it takes to orbit the sun once—is the shortest one of any planet in the solar system, only 88 Earth-days long.

But why does the sun seem to act so strangely in Mercury's sky? From one part of Mercury, as you have seen, it would appear to bob up and down before actually rising and setting. From another part of Mercury, at "noontime," you would see the sun stop, back up for "days," and stop again, before going on its way! And from other parts of the planet, the sun would do equally weird things.

The reason for this is that Mercury has an odd combination of rotation or spin (59 Earth-days), movement around the sun, and shape of orbit that no other planet has. It rotates three times during every two times it goes around the sun. In other words, it has only three days during every two of its years! It has a daylight period— the time when the sun is in the sky—that's as long as one of its years (88 Earth-days) and a nighttime period of the same length. And its orbit is extremely elliptical in shape, like an egg. This causes Mercury to be closer to the sun at times during the daylight period, which makes the sun look bigger. It's farther away at other times, which makes the sun then look smaller. And when Mercury is closest to the sun, it is actually moving around the sun faster than it is rotating. All these things team up to make it seem as if the sun is doing odd tricks.

Of course you couldn't actually stand on the surface of Mercury to watch the sun do its stunts. During the time each side of Mercury faces the sun, the facing side gets more than three times hotter than boiling water! However, when the side that has been facing the sun turns to face the cold darkness of space, the heat soon seeps away and the surface cools to a frigid -280°F. Mercury has hardly any atmosphere to scatter the sunlight as Earth's atmosphere does, which is why its sky is always black.

The surface of Mercury is very much like the surface of Earth's moon. It is all bare rock pitted with billions of craters of all sizes—from tiny pinhead-size holes to enormous ones many miles wide. However, Mercury does not have as many large craters as the moon does.

These craters were all caused by many objects, large and small, that came streaking out of space to slam into Mercury's surface. This probably happened billions of years ago, not long after Mercury was formed. The objects were almost certainly chunks of rock, but exactly what caused them isn't known. They may have been small fragments formed the same time as the planets and their moons, and those chunks closest to Mercury were pulled in by its gravity. Or, they may have been part of a single object, such as a comet, that once passed too close to the sun and was broken into small pieces by gravity. Those pieces would have then caused a "shower" to rain down on all the inner planets (Mercury, Venus, Earth, and Mars) as well as on the moons of Earth and Mars—for there are craters on all these planets. However, it's possible that Mercury's craters were caused at a different time and by something other than what caused the craters on the other planets. Astronomers aren't sure.

It looks as if after the "bombardment" of Mercury was over, hot lava from inside the planet seeped up out of the holes and cracks that had been made on the surface by the meteoroids. The lava spread to form broad plains on parts of Mercury's surface. The surface of Mercury also has many long stretches of steep cliffs running for hundreds of miles. So, altogether, Mercury seems a gloomy and forbidding place—bare rock cliffs, bare rock plains, and billions of big and little craters, all beneath a sky that stays pitch black even when the sun is up. It is extremely doubtful that there could be any kind of life on the planet.

Although the outside of Mercury is very much like the outside of Earth's moon, the inside of Mercury is probably a lot like the Earth's inside. Mercury probably has a large core, or ball, of hot, liquid iron at its center, as Earth has. Scientists think this because Mercury has a density about the same as Earth's. It also has a magnetic field, as Earth has, which is caused by its iron core. Thus, if you took a compass to Mercury, the compass needle would point in one direction, as happens on Earth. This *wouldn't* happen on Earth's moon.

Mercury is much smaller than Earth, less than half as big. Its gravity is only about a third as strong as the gravity on Earth. You could jump about three times higher on Mercury than you can here.

When Mercury's orbit brings it to its closest point to Earth, it is about 49 million miles away from us—not really very far compared to some of the other planets. But because Mercury is so close to the sun, it is usually out of sight for us at night, just as the sun is. It can only be clearly seen without a telescope at certain times of the year: when it appears very low in the eastern sky just before sunrise and when it appears very low in the western sky just after sunset. Because it appears and disappears rather quickly, it seems to be darting about in the sky. This is how it got its name. It is named after the Roman god Mercury, the messenger for all the other gods, who, according to the belief of the Romans, could run swiftly through the sky.

Roman god Mercury

Mariner 10

Venus—CLOUDS AND LIGHTNING

ASTRONOMERS, for a good many years, thought of the planet Venus—the second planet of the solar system—as Earth's "twin sister." The two planets seemed much alike. They are nearly the same size, with Venus being only 405 miles smaller in diameter. Their gravity is nearly the same—if you weigh 100 pounds on Earth, you'd weigh about 10 pounds less on Venus. And their density is nearly the same—a chunk of Venus, if brought to Earth, would weigh about the same as a same-size chunk of Earth. So the two worlds seem to have much in common.

However, until recently, astronomers couldn't tell what Venus was like, for it lies wrapped in an extremely thick blanket of clouds. What those clouds were, and what lay beneath them, was a mystery. Scientists could only guess.

At about the beginning of this century, it was thought that the clouds of Venus were probably formed of water vapor, as Earth's clouds are. And inasmuch as they are so thick, it seemed as if there must be a good deal of moisture on the planet's surface. Some astronomers felt it must be a world of warm, swampy forests, much like the earth was during the time of the dinosaurs.

Writers of science fiction stories made up tales of journeys to Venus in which travelers from Earth found dinosaurlike monsters or froglike "people" living in vast swamps.

Later, better scientific instruments showed there was practically *no* water vapor on Venus. What could the clouds be?

Dust, said some astronomers, offering the idea that Venus was a dry, warm, desert world, swept by great winds that piled clouds of dust in the sky. Other scientists suggested the clouds might be made of carbon dioxide gas, which would mean the surface of Venus was probably one enormous ocean. Still other scientists felt the clouds were a sort of thick smog and the planet covered with an ocean of oil!

Today, we no longer have to guess about the surface and clouds of Venus. Data from American and Russian space probes sent to the planet in the 1970s and radar pictures taken from Earth have shown us Venus.

Imagine a desert. Not a desert of golden rolling sand dunes, but a horribly bleak, parched, barren landscape marred and scarred by jagged cracks and splits. In many places lie clusters of sharp-edged boulders. In some places, the desert is gashed by great chasms, and at least one of them

THE SURFACE OF VENUS

makes the earth's mighty Grand Canyon look like a puny ditch! This chasm is 900 miles long, 175 miles wide, and some 3 miles deep—truly enormous!

This isn't a bright, sun-drenched place like the Sahara or Gobi deserts of Earth. The sky overhead is a continuous sea of thick clouds through which sunlight shows only as a dim, red glow. If you could stand on this desert, you couldn't see any farther than about a mile in any direction. But you would be able to see your near surroundings quite well, for the sky is filled with the constant flare of as many as 25 bolts of lightning every second, providing a lucid glow. Unending thunder shakes the air!

And this is not just an ordinary hot desert, like Earth's Sahara with its average summertime temperature of 90-110°F. This desert *sizzles* at a temperature of about 900°F—more than four times hotter than boiling water! Nor is this desert merely one spot on the planet, as the Sahara is one place on the face of the earth. This desert covers the whole surface of Venus!

As for the atmosphere of Venus, it really *is* a sort of smog, as some scientists thought years ago. The "air" is composed mainly of heavy, smothering carbon dioxide gas, and the clouds are formed of tiny droplets of sulfuric acid, an acid that can dissolve many substances, including metals.

There are also several *puzzling* gases in Venus' atmosphere—gases no one expected to find there. They are gases of the sort that were probably in the huge cloud from which the sun and planets were formed, and scientists can't yet account for why so much

of them should be left in Venus' atmosphere, when they're almost gone from the atmospheres of Earth and Mars. Was Venus, or its atmosphere, formed in a different way from Earth and Mars?

Tremendous winds roar through the upper part of Venus' atmosphere. The winds at the planet's surface, where the air is surprisingly "clean," blow at a speed of only about 2 miles an hour, which is just a light breeze on Earth, but above the surface the winds grow stronger and stronger. At about 40 miles above the desert, the wind rushes through the thick clouds at an incredible speed of some 265 miles an hour. Not even the wildest hurricane ever to howl on Earth blew as hard as that! Because of these tremendous winds (and other influences) the upper atmosphere of Venus seems to be constantly swirling around the planet about 50 times faster than Venus rotates. Scientists are not sure why Venus' winds are so violent—perhaps from the heat of the sun acting on the thick clouds.

Probably the combination of sun's heat and clouds causes Venus to be as dreadfully hot as it is. To begin with, because it is so much closer to the sun, Venus gets about twice as much sunlight as the earth does. So even though much of this light and heat is reflected back off into space by the thick clouds, the amount of it that's kept is still just about as much as Earth gets altogether. And scientists think that most of this plentiful amount of heat that reaches Venus' surface is then "trapped" there by the thick roof of clouds. Thus, the surface has heated up and stays hot.

As you can see, the old idea that Venus is Earth's "twin sister" is far, far from the truth. Venus is about as much like the earth as a snake is like a puppy!

Since 1975, we have learned more about Venus' surface and atmosphere than scientists had known for hundreds of years previously. But there is still much to find out. Radar pictures made of Venus seem to show that the Venusian desert contains ranges of rough mountains and live volcanoes. This could mean that portions of Venus' surface may be shaken by earthquakes and racked by volcanic eruptions. The pictures also show that some parts of Venus appear to be completely different from anything on Earth. What caused these strange features? We will probably know about all this before *you* are much older.

Venus is about 67 million miles from the sun and about 25 million miles from Earth at its closest. Inasmuch as it is so close to the sun, Venus takes a shorter time to move around the sun than Earth does. A Venus-year is equal to only 225 Earth-days. However, Venus *rotates* much more slowly than Earth does, so a day on Venus is equal to 243 Earth-days! In other words, a full Venus-day (one complete rotation period) is longer than a whole Venus year! A night on Venus lasts for 58½ Earth-days.

Venus not only rotates very slowly, it is also the only planet in the solar system to rotate "backward." Every other planet rotates in the same direction in which it moves around the sun, but Venus rotates in the opposite direction. Thus, if the sun could be seen on Venus, it would rise in the west and set in the east, instead of the other way around, as on Earth.

Scientists do not agree on how to account for Venus' "backward" rotation. Some think Venus may once have been struck by a huge object that stopped its normal rotation and caused the planet to start rotating very slowly in the opposite direction. Others think maybe Venus was formed by large pieces that came together with such an impact that the new planet moved only very slowly, and in the "wrong" direction.

Venus is usually easy to find, for it's the very brightest thing in the sky and can be clearly seen without a telescope. In fact, at certain times it is so bright it can be seen in the daytime, which has caused many people who don't know what it is to report it as an UFO. At certain times of year, when Venus is moving toward Earth, it is the first "star" to show up in the western sky in the evening, before sunset. At other times, when it is moving away from Earth, it is the last "star" to fade from the sky in the morning. Because of this, astronomers of long ago thought it was two different stars, and gave it names that meant "morning star" and "evening star." Later, they found it was really just one object, and because of its bright beauty they named it after Venus, the Roman goddess of beauty and love. But if they had known what it is really like—a harsh, super-hot desert, illuminated by dim red sunlight and unending lightning flashes, lying beneath miles of thick, smoglike clouds torn by wild winds—they would probably have given it a very different name!

19

Venus, Roman goddess of love

The Moon—EARTH'S COMPANION

LOOKING at the surface of the moon is like looking back through time—at the surface of the earth as it must have looked billions of years ago, not long after it was formed!

The earth is an ever-changing world. During its billions of years of life, whole mountain ranges have been thrust up then slowly worn away by wind and rain. Seas have changed position. The continents have changed shape. All these changes have wiped out the record of our world's earliest days. The oldest rocks we can find on Earth are about 3½ billion years old, but the earth is a good billion years older than that. The first billion years of our history have been "erased" by wind, rain, earthquakes, volcanic eruptions, continental drift—the activities of a *living* world.

But Earth's closest neighbor in space, the moon, is a dead world without wind, rain, seas, or changing continents. It has hardly changed at all in many billions of years. And so, by studying it, we can learn something of what our planet was like in its early days. Because the moon is so close to us—only about 240 thousand miles away—we can study it quite well. We have even been able to visit it and to bring some of its rocks and soil back with us to Earth.

Shortly after the earth and moon were formed, they were bombarded by a great "rain" of *planetesimals*—chunks of rock formed at about the same time and out of the same gas and dust as the inner planets of the solar system. These chunks of rock were pulled by gravity toward the planets nearest them, causing the smaller objects to come rushing out of space to slam into the surface, making bowl-shaped pits. We know that many millions of these planetesimals slammed into the earth billions of years ago, but now all traces of them are long gone.

On the moon, however, the traces of some of those planetesimals (and of other objects that have crashed into the moon during the last few billion years) are still plain to see. The moon has thousands of billions of craters about a foot wide. It has about half a million craters a mile or more wide. Many craters are 10 to 15 miles wide, and some are much more. The biggest crater is about 700 miles wide. These craters are scattered over the moon's whole surface —some inside others, some on top of others, some joined together in clusters. And this is how the surface of the earth probably

1969 ASTRONAUTS
LAND ON THE MOON.

looked a few million years after it had been formed and after it cooled.

Many of the mountains of the moon, some of which are as high as Earth's highest, are actually the sides of giant craters. What a sight it must have been when a gigantic chunk of rock many hundreds of miles wide came crashing into the moon, causing a tremendous flare of heat, smashing itself to pieces, creating an enormous hole, and throwing up masses of rock all around to form *mountains!* Yet, despite that titanic impact, that incredible mountain-making smash, there would not have been a sound! For the moon has no atmosphere to carry sound waves.

The mountains of the moon form highlands, and there are also lowlands—broad, flat plains. Lowlands make the grayish patches you can see on the moon's face. Most were probably formed well over 3 billion years ago when a gigantic object crashed into the moon, forming a great "basin." Hot lava flowed up out of the moon's interior, filled the basin, and cooled into solid rock. Long thin canyons, called rilles, cut the moon's surface. Some are cracks in the surface, others were probably caused by flowing lava.

Men have walked on the face of the moon, so we know exactly what it's like. The landscape is pale brownish gray, and what look like distant mountains and hills may actually be the sides of craters. The moon's plains are covered with powdery soil made up of ground rock and bits of glass. This soil was formed by the billions of rocky objects that have smashed into the moon, grinding themselves and the moon's surface to powder. The heat of those impacts changed bits of rock into glass.

Because the moon has no atmosphere to either carry sound waves or to scatter light waves, its sky is never bright as Earth's is. Instead the moon's sky is always black and filled with stars. But often there is something other than stars in the moon's sky. There is the awesome and beautiful sight of our world, Earth, hanging in the blackness like a huge blue and white marble, bright with reflected sunlight.

The bright light that glows from a full moon in our sky is also reflected sunlight. Bright though it seems, the moon, like all planets, has no light of its own. Some of the sunlight that falls upon its surface is reflected back into space, making it seem to glow, just as the earth glows in the moon's sky.

The moon moves in orbit around Earth, held in place by gravity, just as Earth moves in orbit around the sun. The moon's orbit takes it completely around the earth in about a month. If you watch it nightly during this time, you will see it appear to gradually change shape. It grows from a thin, curved bow to a half circle, to a full circle, back to a bow again, then it seems to vanish altogether. Long ago, people called the period of time from when the moon first appeared as a bow to when it vanished a "moon." Our period of time called a month is based on this meaning of "moon."

These changes of the moon that take place during a month are called phases.

While half of the moon is always in sunlight, just as half of the earth always is, we can often only see a portion of the moon's sunlit side from the earth. When the moon is between the sun and the earth, we can't see the moon's sunlit side at all, and that's when the moon seems to have vanished. But as the moon's orbit carries it around the earth, more and more of the sunlit side can be seen. When the moon is halfway around us, we can see the whole side of it that is in full sunlight—the glowing circle we call a full moon. And this is how the moon's phases happen.

It's another odd fact that the side of the moon we see glowing with reflected sunlight is always the *same* side. While the earth spins around and shows all of itself to the moon, the moon has never shown more than about half of itself to Earth. The pull of Earth's gravity keeps the same side of the moon always facing us as it moves around us. The moon spins, but it makes only one complete spin during the entire time it takes to go around us, and this works out to keep us from ever seeing its other side.

And so, for hundreds of years, people wondered what the other side of the moon was like. In 1959, we began to find out. A Russian space vessel passed over the moon's other side and took pictures that were sent back to Earth by television. Since then, many other pictures have been taken, and we now know exactly what the moon's other side is like. It really isn't much different from the side we can see, except that it has fewer plains and its craters have a smoother, more worn look.

Much as we know about the moon, we don't quite know where it came from. Scientists aren't quite sure whether it's Earth's "baby," Earth's "prisoner," or whether it's Earth's "baby brother!"

One idea is that when Earth was still quite new and hot, the gravity of the sun, tugging at the soft planet, caused a part of it to bulge out. Slowly, the pull of gravity plus the spinning of the earth made the bulge stretch out and break off, forming the moon. This would mean that the moon is Earth's "baby."

Another idea is that the moon is a planet, formed at about the same time as Earth, that circled around the sun. However, its orbit brought it close to Earth and because it is so much smaller than Earth—only about a fourth as big—the larger planet's gravity grabbed ahold of it and pulled it into a new orbit around us. This would make it actually Earth's "prisoner."

A third idea, one most astronomers think is more likely than the other two, is that the moon was formed just about where it is now and probably very soon after the earth was formed. The earth was probably still surrounded by rock and dust that formed a disk around it. Much of the matter in this disk collected together to form the moon. If the moon was formed this way, you could say that it's Earth's "baby brother." However, scientists still have to learn a good deal more about the moon before they can be completely sure how it came to be.

third quarter   first quarter

east   west

waning crescent   full moon   waxing crescent

suggestion of 21st century Mars landing

Mars—RED PLANET

THE SOLAR SYSTEM'S fourth planet, Mars, shines with a pink twinkle in Earth's night sky, and seen through a telescope it has a reddish orange color. So, for hundreds of years it has been known as the Red Planet. And when we sent a spacecraft to Mars to take pictures of its surface, we discovered that it truly *is* a red planet—a world of rust red deserts, red-hued volcanoes, red brown canyons, and even a bright salmon-colored daytime sky!

Mars is very different from either bleak Mercury with its cloudless, windless, everlastingly black sky, or from parched Venus with its thick veil of clouds. In many ways, Mars is much like Earth. If you could stand on the surface of Mars, you might well think you were standing in one of the dry, mountainous desert parts of the southwestern United States. You would see a reddish brown plain, dotted with countless boulders, stretched out beneath a pinkish orange sky that might contain a small white or bluish cloud or two. You might see a towering mountain in the distance. Or you might find yourself in a rocky canyon.

But some of the things on the surface of Mars seem to be on a much grander scale than similar things on Earth. There are gigantic volcanoes on the Red Planet that make our biggest mountains seem puny by comparison! The biggest of these volcanoes, Olympus Mons, is 360 miles wide and 15 miles high—two and a half times taller than Mt. Everest, Earth's tallest mountain! There is also a canyon on Mars that rivals the giant canyon on Venus. Called Valles Marineris, it is over 3,000 miles long—about as long as the whole continent of North America is wide!

The winds of Mars, too, seem to blow sometimes on a grander scale than the winds of Earth. While they normally blow at speeds of about 10 miles an hour, it appears as if they can reach speeds of more than 100 miles an hour. On Earth this would be a hurricane. These strong winds pick up tons of Mars' reddish brown soil and carry it in clouds over the entire planet. Particles of this reddish dust, hanging in the air, give the Martian sky its salmon color.

The surface of Mars is dotted with craters. Mars' atmosphere isn't thick enough to burn up most of the meteoroids that have crashed into it, as Earth's thick atmosphere does. It can burn up most of the smaller ones, however, so although Mars has far

MARS' LANDSCAPE

Mars' explorers will need oxygen helmets.

more craters than Earth has, it has fewer craters, and fewer small craters, than either Mercury or the moon (which, of course, have no protection at all against the many objects that come hurtling in from space).

If you stood on a Martian plain in the wintertime—for Mars has a winter and summer just as Earth has—you would see broad patches of white frost at the feet of many of the boulders on the plain. In the summer, these patches would be gone.

But, winter or summer, you would have to be wearing very warm clothing, for Mars is *cold*. During a summer day, average temperatures range from about 25 degrees below zero to nighttime temperatures of 130 degrees below zero! You would also need an oxygen-supplying helmet such as astronauts wore on the moon, for there isn't enough oxygen in Mars' thin atmosphere to keep you alive. And if you grew thirsty you would be out of luck, for there is no water in liquid form on the Red Planet.

However, while there is no flowing water on Mars now, there was probably water there at one time. Close-up pictures of Mars taken by a spacecraft show what appear to be dry riverbeds—long, winding grooves that look as if they could only have been made by the movement of rivers. And there is frozen water, ice, at Mars' north and south poles, just as there is on Earth. These big sheets of ice at the Martian poles show signs of having been melted in the past, perhaps about 100 million years ago. This must mean that Mars not only once had water, it was also *warm*. Many scientists think Mars may now be in an ice age, as

Earth was in about 10 thousand years ago, and could warm up again. Then the ice at the poles would once more melt, and again there would be rivers and perhaps lakes on the Red Planet.

Because Mars *is* so much like Earth, and because it may once have been warm and wet, many scientists have until recently felt there might be living things on Mars. In fact, for about a hundred years, many people seriously believed there might be *intelligent* living creatures there!

The reason for this was that in 1877, an Italian astronomer named Giovanni Schiaparelli, looking at Mars through a telescope, saw what looked to him like a number of long straight lines on its surface. He thought they might be riverbeds and named them *cannali,* an Italian word meaning "channels" or "grooves." Because "cannali" sounds so much like "canals," most people thought that Schiaparelli had said that he'd seen *canals* on Mars. Now, of course, a canal, such as the Panama or the Suez, can only be made by intelligent beings. And so a great many people, some of them scientists, began to think there might be intelligent beings on Mars.

Also, many astronomers studying Mars noticed that its surface appeared to change at certain times. Parts of it grew darker, stayed dark for several months, then lightened again. This looked as if perhaps *plants* might be growing on large areas of Mars during the summer and then dying away during winter, as many Earth plants do. This, too, strengthened the belief in life on Mars.

Earth
(comparative size)

26

Mars

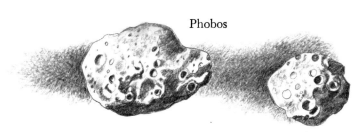

Phobos

Deimos

But today, we know that any channels on Mars weren't dug by anyone; they are natural formations like our Grand Canyon. And the regular darkening and lightening of Mars' surface is caused by great sandstorms blowing, often for months at a time, across the Martian landscape. So the idea of intelligent life on Mars has been abandoned.

Until very recently, however, many scientists thought there might be tiny, microscopic living things such as bacteria in the Martian soil. The Viking spacecrafts that landed on Mars in the late 1970s were equipped to make tests to see if there were living things in the soil. The results of the tests were puzzling. To some scientists they seemed to show that, while the soil of Mars is oddly different from that of Earth, there are no living things in it. Other scientists think the tests showed that there *are* microbes in the Martian soil. More tests will have to be made before we can tell for sure.

Mars has two moons, neither of which is as large and handsome as Earth's moon. Phobos is larger than Deimos, but both of these moons are judged to be smaller than 10 miles wide and black in color. Both moons are just battered, rocky chunks covered with craters. They may be the remains of a larger, more nicely rounded moon broken up by the rain of planetesimals that long ago smashed into all the inner planets. It is more likely, however, that they may be two of the tiny planets called asteroids that were captured by Mars' gravity long ago.

Both Deimos and Phobos are much closer to Mars than our moon is to us. In fact, if Phobos were just slightly closer, it would have been broken up by Mars' gravity, and its pieces would form a ring around the Red Planet.

Mars is a smaller planet than Earth, only a little more than half the size of our world. At its closest point to us it is about 35 million miles away, the second closest planet after Venus. Its day is almost the same length as ours. Because it is so much farther from the sun than we are, it takes longer to make its orbit, so its year is almost twice as long as ours. Because of its reddish twinkle, it was long ago named after Mars, the Romans' red and bloody god of war. And its moons are named after two of war's followers—"fear" and "terror" (or "panic").

With its atmosphere, its winds, its volcanoes, and its polar ice caps, Mars is not a dead, unchanging world like Mercury or the moon. It is an *active* planet where things can happen! And it is not a frightfully hot and inhospitable place like Venus. It is a planet humans could visit and explore. Very likely they *will* explore it in your lifetime!

Roman god Mars

27

suggestion of a 21st century spacecraft

Earth and Jupiter
(comparative size)

Jupiter—NEARLY A STAR

JUPITER, biggest of all the planets—big enough to hold 1,000 planets the size of Earth within itself—was nearly the solar system's second sun.

The fifth planet away from the sun, Jupiter is completely different from the first four. Instead of being a ball of rock and metal as they are, it is a gigantic ball of *liquid*. This liquid is actually mostly hydrogen gas that has been squeezed together so tightly by gravity it has become a hot liquid. Thus, Jupiter is made out of the same material as the sun. And if it had a little more mass—the material of which it is formed—it could have become a star, like the sun. If its mass had been great enough, its center would have been squeezed together so tightly it could have become a thermonuclear furnace, like the center of the sun. But, as it is, Jupiter became simply a very large planet, shining with reflected light instead of with light of its own. As one astronomer has said, Jupiter is "a star that failed."

At its closest point to Earth, Jupiter is about 390 million miles away from us. Its year is about 12 Earth-years long. Because it spins very rapidly—faster than any of the other planets—its day is only 9 hours and 55 minutes long. The gravity of Jupiter is much greater than the gravity of Earth. If you weigh 100 pounds on Earth, you'd weigh 287 pounds standing on Jupiter—if there were a place to stand on it.

Although Jupiter is a ball of gas compressed into liquid, it may have a molten core of heavier elements (rock and metal) at its center. Surrounding this core is a layer of liquid hydrogen about 33 thousand miles deep. Beyond the liquid "surface" begins the atmosphere. The change from liquid to atmosphere is probably so gradual, it would be hard to tell exactly where the liquid "surface" stops and the atmosphere begins. Scientists generally say the change is made several hundred miles under the cloud tops.

Moving up from the "surface," first comes a layer of water droplets that, higher up, freezes into an icy mist. Then come bands of icy crystals and clouds made up mostly of frozen ammonia. (Ammonia is the eye-smarting, nose-searing liquid chemical used for cleaning grease off kitchen floors and cabinets.) More than 8 miles above the cloud tops is a thin layer of hydrogen gas and other gases.

All this talk about icy clouds makes it

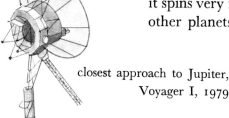

closest approach to Jupiter,
Voyager I, 1979

JUPITER AS SEEN FROM A MOON

Cassini

sound as if Jupiter is a very cold place. Actually, it isn't. Jupiter *gives off* more heat than it absorbs from the sun, which probably means that its center is *hot*—about six times hotter than the surface of the sun. This heat is probably left over from the tremendous heat created when the planet was first formed. Now, the heat is slowly "leaking" out.

Jupiter's thick, cloudy atmosphere is spectacular. It abounds with colors—red, brown, yellow, orange, blue, and white. And these colorful clouds don't placidly drift, like the clouds of Earth do; they rush, swirl, and collide, driven by winds that blow at speeds of more than 300 miles an hour! Dozens of giant storms are always raging in Jupiter's atmosphere, and most of them are as much as 6,000 miles wide. Enormous "super" lightning bolts flare above the cloud tops. Imagine tremendous hurricanes and tornadoes, stretched all the way around the Earth, rushing in different directions and lit by frequent titanic flashes of lightning, and you'll have an idea of what the "weather" on Jupiter is like!

Nor do Jupiter's storms rage for just a few hours, or even for a few days. One of them has been going on for *centuries!* It is like a giant whirlpool in the planet's atmosphere a little below its equator. Through a telescope it is a reddish, oval-shaped spot that stands out against the rest of the planet like a big red eye. It is a gigantic, 20,000-mile-wide hurricane—long and wide enough to hold three planets the size of Earth. It swirls counterclockwise and reaches a height of about 8 miles above Jupiter's ammonia

clouds, while the planet's other swift-moving clouds split to flow above and below it.

This spot on Jupiter's face was first seen through a telescope in 1665 by an Italian astronomer named Cassini, and astronomers stared at it in puzzlement for 300 years without knowing what it was. They named it the Great Red Spot, and came up with all sorts of ideas as to what it might be. At first, it was thought to be the mouth of a huge volcano that was poking up through the clouds. But then, astronomers noticed that the spot moved, so it obviously couldn't be a volcano. Very well, then, was it perhaps a new moon that was forming—a chunk of the planet that was somehow being torn loose? Was it perhaps a kind of motionless wave that had somehow formed in the cloudy atmosphere? It wasn't until 1973, after the space probe Pioneer 10 swung past Jupiter, sending back information and pictures, that the mystery of the Great Red Spot was solved.

Jupiter has several other features besides its awesome storms and size. It is a *ringed* planet, surrounded by a very thin, dark ring of what may be dust, pebbles, and boulders that perhaps never formed into a moon or perhaps are the remains of a moon that got too close to Jupiter and was tugged to pieces. Jupiter is also surrounded by a doughnut-shaped ring of extremely hot gas with a powerful electric charge!

At least thirteen moons orbit the huge globe of Jupiter—more, as far as we yet know, than circle any other planet. Two, Ganymede and Callisto, are actually planet size, being slightly larger than Mercury.

Galileo Galilei (1564–1642) discovered Jupiter's first four moons.

Two others, Io and Europa, are about the size of Earth's moon. The other nine are all quite small, ranging in diameter from 5 miles to 100 miles or so. The smallest moon, Leda, is less than 6 miles wide and was first discovered in 1974. It was the newest moon to be found in the solar system until the discovery of Pluto's moon in mid-1978. Some scientists think Jupiter may have a tiny fourteenth moon, a moon we haven't yet been able to verify.

Io, closest to Jupiter of the four large moons, is an orange red and gold ball that looks, as some astronomers have said, like a pizza! To many scientists, Io is the most exciting thing in the solar system, for it is the only planet besides Earth, as far as we yet know, that has *active* volcanoes that frequently erupt and throw hot ash, gases, and lava onto the planet's surface! These volcanoes seem to erupt with much greater force than any of Earth's volcanoes. Io also apparently has "lakes" of molten lava. Thus, it is obviously an active, *changing* world, perhaps much like Earth was in its early days. The picture of Io that scientists have worked out is a world of reddish brown plains, plateaus, glowing lakes of lava, spitting volcanoes, perhaps a towering range of mountains, and a sky that's often filled with a yellowish glow!

The second farthest moon, Europa, is a pale orange color and covered with many streaks apparently thousands of miles long. It seems to be made mostly of rocky material covered with ice. Ganymede, the third-farthest moon, is grayish brown in color and is about half rock and half water and ice. Its surface is covered with ridges and crisscrossed lines that scientists think may have been caused by quakes inside the planet.

The farthest large moon, Callisto, is brown and pocked and pitted with a great many craters, like Mercury and Earth's moon. It, too, seems to be about half rocky material and half water and ice. There are spots on Callisto's surface that look like frozen waves, and one large, smooth basin surrounded by ridges that looks like frozen ripples of the kind made by dropping a stone into water. Scientists think perhaps this odd formation was caused when a huge meteorite slammed into Callisto and went through the ice. A huge shock wave from this might have caused ripples and ridges in the frozen (-200°F) surface.

Giant Jupiter surrounded by its 13 moons is like a mighty king, surrounded by admiring courtiers. It was well named, after the Roman god Jupiter, who was the king and the mightiest of all the Roman gods.

Roman god Jupiter

Saturn—BRIGHT RINGS

SATURN, the solar system's sixth planet, is a fantastic world! It's a giant, ten times bigger than Earth—but it would *float* in water! It is surrounded by awesome shining rings made out of billions of "hailstones!" It has a collection of moons that includes some "snowballs," a moon with one side seemingly very different from the other, and a giant moon wrapped in strange red clouds that just *may* be able to have things living on it!

Saturn is about 793 million miles away from us, but it can easily be seen without a telescope. It's brighter than most stars. Its orbit carries it around the sun in a year as long as 29½ Earth-years, but because it spins very rapidly, its day is about only 10 Earth-hours long. It is formed of the same material as Jupiter, mostly hydrogen gas. The outer portion of the gas forms a thick, cloudy atmosphere miles and miles deep. Farther down, the gas is probably squeezed into a thick layer of liquid many miles deep, and beneath that it may form a thick layer of sludgy ices many miles deep. The very center of the planet is probably a ball of rock or metal thousands of miles wide. The center is so hot it may be a liquid.

Like Jupiter, Saturn gives off more heat than it gets from the sun. This probably is heat that built up when the planet was formed and is now slowly "leaking away." However, Saturn isn't as warm as Jupiter is. Its temperature near the cloud tops is about -290° F., which is far colder than Jupiter. Thus, it's rather doubtful that anything could be living on Saturn.

Despite its gigantic size, Saturn is a very light planet, less dense than Jupiter, and far less dense than Earth. It weighs only about as much as a piece of cork its size would weigh. In fact, if there were a sea somewhere big enough to hold it, Saturn would float!

Saturn's thick atmosphere is streaked with broad, dark bands like those on Jupiter, but Saturn has no permanent marks such as Jupiter's Red Spot. However, mysterious white patches sometimes appear in its atmosphere. One, seen in 1933, was a large oval spot on the planet's equator. It was about 15,000 miles wide when it first appeared, but it quickly grew wider during a period of several weeks, stretching out into a band. It later disappeared. A few more much smaller white spots have been seen since, but they also soon vanished. Some astronomers think these white

astronomers
observing
Saturn's rings

patches may be caused by something like an eruption or explosion down on Saturn's "surface." This disturbance may send a cloud of some kind of material up into the atmosphere, giving the whitish color. But what might cause such an eruption is a mystery.

The wonderful rings forming circles around Saturn can't be seen without a telescope, so no one knew about them until telescopes were invented several hundred years ago. For a long time, astronomers weren't at all sure what the rings were. Today, we know they are made up of billions of little chunks of ice and "debris," almost like hailstones, or perhaps pieces of rock covered with ice. These icy chunks are probably from less than an inch to more than a foot wide and circle around Saturn just as the moon circles around Earth. Sunlight reflecting off the ice makes the rings bright enough to be easily seen with a small telescope.

There are four of these icy rings, one inside another. They surround Saturn at its equator. The rings are about only ½ mile deep, so a fast-moving spacecraft going straight down through a ring would only be among the icy particles for an instant. But the rings extend outward from Saturn for many thousands of miles—about as much as two-thirds of the distance from Earth to the moon.

The outermost ring is about 10,000 miles wide. About 1,700 miles of space is between it and the next ring, which is guessed to be 17,000 miles wide. The third ring is just about 16,000 miles wide; there is a distance

of from 7,000 to 9,000 miles between it and the beginning of Saturn's upper atmosphere. The third ring is much dimmer than the other two, being almost transparent. Apparently, the icy chunks that form it are much less numerous and farther apart than those in the bright outer rings. The fourth ring, which is much closer to Saturn's atmosphere, is even dimmer. Scientists think there may be a fifth, very dim ring outside all the others.

There are several ideas on how the rings came to be. One is that the icy chunks are tiny planetoids that formed at the same time as Saturn and the rest of the planets. Another idea is that the icy chunks are the remains of a moon that was somehow pulled too close to Saturn and was broken up by the big planet's gravity. Still another idea is that the chunks are the remains of a moon and a comet which collided and were smashed to bits. We simply don't know.

In addition to its rings, Saturn has ten known moons, and some astronomers think there may be more small moons yet to be discovered. Saturn's moons are a rather curious collection, some of which are very different from others.

Three of them, named Mimas, Enceladus, and Tethys, are probably nothing more than dirty "snowballs" made mostly of ice and frozen ammonia. Tethys is about 750 miles wide, Enceladus and Mimas are about 370 and 320 miles wide, respectively. Scientists do not all agree on the moons' sizes; the sizes are hard to pinpoint.

The moons called Rhea and Dione,

which are about 1,100 and 800 miles wide respectively, are about as dense as Earth's moon, and are probably made of rock. The moon called Iapetus, which is about 800 miles wide, is rather mysterious, because one side of it seems to be about six times brighter than .the other side. Astronomers wonder if this means the bright side is different from the other, and, if so, in what way. Perhaps one side is icy and the other is not, but why should that be?

One of Saturn's smallest moons, Phoebe, which is only about 190 miles in diameter, may not be a moon at all, but may be an asteroid whose orbit brought it so close to Saturn that it was captured by the big planet's gravity. It is much, much farther away from Saturn than any of the other moons, and hardly seems to "belong" with them.

But the moon that is of greatest interest to astronomers is the moon named Titan. For one thing, it is the largest of all moons in the solar system, being about 3,500 miles wide—really, the size of a respectable planet. It is nearly as large as Mars and larger than Mercury and Pluto, the ninth planet. For another thing, Titan has a thick, cloudy atmosphere probably made up mostly of methane gas. We often call methane marsh gas, because it sometimes forms near swamps and marshes. Methane and other substances cause Titan's thick atmosphere to be reddish brown. Its sky must be the color of dried blood! For still another thing, Titan is warm for its distance from the sun. It should be colder. Scientists think perhaps Titan's thick atmosphere traps and holds much of the sunlight that reaches the satellite, thus heating up its surface.

Some scientists have suggested that there may be active volcanoes on Titan that often erupt and throw off clouds of gas, water vapor, and liquid rock. And there may also be lakes and ponds of liquid methane and perhaps water on Titan.

Now, all this raises some interesting ideas in the minds of some astronomers. Warmth, an atmosphere, pools of liquid, erupting volcanoes—these are some of the ingredients that could produce life! Some scientists think Titan may be very much like Earth was billions of years ago when, it is believed, life began in the water on our planet's surface. Scientists generally agree life began on Earth as a result of chemical changes that were caused by the warmth, the chemicals in the atmosphere, the eruption of volcanoes, and other things. Perhaps life could also begin in those pools of liquid on Titan! So this big moon of Saturn's is a place many scientists would like to know a lot more about!

Saturn

Uranus

Uranus, Neptune, Pluto—OUTER PLANETS

THE THREE PLANETS that lie out beyond Saturn are all rather mysterious. They are so tremendously far away from us, there is very little we can find out about them. Even the nearest is so dim and distant no one knew it was a planet until about 200 years ago. Up until then, for thousands of years, everyone thought there were only six planets in the solar system. The other two planets are so far away they can only be seen with a powerful telescope—and even then you have to know exactly where to look.

Uranus, the seventh planet of the solar system, is about one billion, 700 million miles away from us at the closest part of its orbit. We can tell it's a big planet, more than four times the size of Earth. It appears to have a thick atmosphere, made up of clouds of ammonia, and it's apparently quite cold. Data tells us that Uranus' day may be 13 Earth-hours, and its year is equal to about 84 Earth-years.

Astronomers who have watched Uranus carefully over long periods of time think they have seen what look like grayish bands and faint spots in its atmosphere. What these markings might be, if they really exist, is unknown. And what the surface of Uranus is like, beneath its cloudy atmosphere, is also unknown. Uranus is probably less dense than Jupiter. Astronomers tend to think it may have a center of hot rock several thousand miles wide surrounded by ices thousands of miles thick.

Until 1977, people thought Saturn was the only ringed planet in the solar system. Some felt that a ringed planet was probably quite rare. But then it was found that Uranus, too, has rings around it. Because they are dark instead of bright like Saturn's rings, Uranus' rings are very hard to see. But there are at least five of them, and perhaps as many as nine. Most are only a few miles deep. Because the rings are dark, scientists are sure they are not ice covered; they may just be thin circles of black, rocky dust.

Uranus also has five moons that can be seen with a telescope, and it may have other, smaller moons still to be discovered. The biggest of Uranus' moons, Titania, is judged to be 1,120 miles wide. The smallest, Miranda, is thought to be 248 miles wide. Nothing much more is known about any of these satellites.

Uranus is named after an ancient Greek sky god. Neptune, the eighth planet, is

36

Roman god Neptune

named after the ancient Roman god of the sea. Neptune's orbit carries it to its closest point to Earth at about two billion, 678 million miles away. Neptune is only a little smaller than Uranus, just about four times the size of Earth. Its year is about 165 Earth-years long and its day is just about 18 Earth-hours in length.

Astronomers think that Neptune is probably much like Uranus. It may have a molten rock core several thousand miles wide, covered by a thick coating of ice thousands of miles deep. It also has a thick atmosphere apparently made up mostly of hydrogen and helium gases. A few faint markings have been reported to be in this atmosphere, but it is not possible to tell anything about them. Neptune has a faintly greenish tint, due to chemicals in its atmosphere. The atmosphere absorbs the red, orange, and yellow rays of the sun, and thus the light reflected back toward us is mainly bluish green. Uranus has such a greenish hue, too.

Neptune has two known moons, Triton and Nereid. Triton is a respectable-size planetoid, about 3,000 miles wide, which is quite a bit bigger than Earth's moon. Nereid is apparently about 370 miles wide. As to what Uranus' moons may be like, no one can say at this time.

Astronomers knew that Neptune existed before they were able to see it. They had noticed that the orbit of Uranus was uneven. Something appeared to be *tugging* at Uranus, pulling it slightly out of the orbit it should have had. Such a tug could only be caused by the gravity of a large "near-by" object. By means of mathematics, astronomers figured out where this object should be, and telescopes were turned toward it. Shortly thereafter, Neptune was found, in the year 1846.

The ninth planet, Pluto, was also suspected before it was seen. Once again, certain oddities in the orbits of Uranus and Neptune caused astronomers to believe there must be another planet, farther out than Neptune, giving a gravitational tug to affect Uranus' and Neptune's orbits. And once again with mathematics astronomers found where the planet must be. But it was not until 1930 that Pluto was actually photographed. It is so far away—four and a half billion miles at its farthest and two billion, 700 million at its nearest—that it's just a speck of light in even today's most powerful telescope. Yet, far away though it is most of the time, once every 248 years its rather odd orbit brings it closer to the sun, for a number of years, than Neptune is.

Pluto surprised astronomers in 1978, because it was found to be much smaller than astronomers had expected it to be, judging from the amount of tug it *seemed* to be giving to Uranus and Neptune. It is the solar system's smallest planet, only about 1,500 miles in diameter. Some scientists think that Pluto is a ball of cold frozen gases and dust, with a rocky core and frozen crust.

Pluto has a tiny moon, just discovered in mid-1978. The moon was named Charon. It is 500 miles in diameter, and nothing is known about what it is made of. Charon is only about 12,000 miles from Pluto's sur-

Plu

Pluto's orbit

other planets' orbits

face, and it moves around Pluto in almost exactly the same amount of time that Pluto spins on its axis—about six Earth-days. Thus, although Charon moves all the way around Pluto as our moon does around us, it would not be "seen" from all parts of the planet. It is always above the same part of Pluto. To understand how this works, imagine you have a small ball stuck to a bigger ball with a long pin. As you turn the larger ball, the little one goes right around with it, always in the same place.

Pluto is named after the Roman god of death and darkness—a fitting name, it seems, for the farthest planet in the dark, cold, most remote part of the solar system. But *is* Pluto actually the farthest planet? Or is there still another world even farther out that hasn't yet been discovered? Many astronomers think so, because Pluto just doesn't seem big enough to be able to cause the tug on Uranus and Neptune. Pluto may have a distant, rather large neighbor—the solar system's tenth planet!

For a short time in 1977, it looked as if Pluto itself might actually *be* the tenth planet. In that year, an astronomer dis-covered a strange small object circling the sun in an orbit between Saturn and Uranus. The object seemed too far out to be an asteroid, and it was definitely not a moon of either Saturn or Uranus, so it looked as if it were nothing less than a newly discovered planet. That would have made it the seventh planet from the sun, shoving Pluto into tenth position. Furthermore, inasmuch as the new object was guessed to be only from 100 to 400 miles in diameter, it would have been the smallest planet in the solar system—a "miniplanet."

However, after further study of the little object, astronomers decided it just didn't fit the role of a planet. But as to what it is, they couldn't quite decide. Scientists know something about its size and orbit period, but not about what it is made of. Some thought it might be the nucleus of a very large comet; others thought it might be a large asteroid that had gone astray and picked up a coating of ice. Whatever it is, like Uranus and Neptune, their moons, and Pluto, it is part of the solar system's outermost family—faint, far, and still most mysterious.

Asteroids—TINY PLANETS

FEBRUARY 12, 1947, a visitor from space landed on the earth.

Its coming was seen by many people in the Russian village of Novopokrovka, in Siberia. Those who chanced to be outdoors on that cloudless winter day were suddenly aware of an unusual brightness in the sky. Looking up, they saw what many of them later described as a ball of light as bright as the sun and about the size of a full moon streaking across the sky, shooting out sparks and leaving a thick, black trail behind. In seconds the object had passed out of sight, heading toward a distant mountain range.

When news of this was sent to the Russian capital of Moscow, a group of astronomers and geologists set out as quickly as possible for the mountains in Siberia where it was thought the object had landed. What these scientists found on one mountain slope was a patch of destruction, roughly 1,500 feet wide, peppered with more than 100 holes, some of which were as much as 75 feet wide and 40 feet deep. The ground around these craters was strewn with chunks of scarred and pitted iron—from big pieces several hundred pounds in weight to tiny motes. Among the trees that clustered the mountainside near the damaged place were a number whose tops had been sliced off, marking the path of the thing that had slammed so violently into the earth.

What was it that had come blazing through the sky and struck the earth on that February day? Well, it had once been nothing less than a tiny planet of the kind known as an asteroid.

Asteroids are members of the solar system, just as Earth and the other planets are. The name *asteroid* means "starlike," so it isn't a very good name, as asteroids aren't a bit like stars. A better name by which they are often called is "planetoid." This means "planetlike." And they are miniature planets—little lumps of rock and metal that circle the sun between the orbits of Mars and Jupiter in a great swarm called the asteroid belt. Thousands of them have been seen, but there may be many millions. The largest, named Ceres, has the modestly respectable size of about 480 miles in diameter, just about the size of the whole country of Spain. About twenty others are at least 100 miles in diameter. But most are probably only a few feet wide, and many millions must be no bigger than pebbles.

Ceres and Spain
(comparative size)

METEOR CRASHING TO EARTH

Where did this orbiting rock heap, the asteroid belt, come from? Most astronomers think the asteroids were formed at the same time as the rest of the solar system, and when they were formed there were probably far fewer of them than there are now. They may have started out as a number of planets all quite a bit smaller than Earth's moon. Or they may have been pieces of what "tried" to become a single large planet but were kept from coming together because of the tug of giant Jupiter's gravity. At any rate, they have slowly been broken up into smaller and smaller pieces over the billions of years of their existence.

The reason for this steady breakup is that asteroids frequently collide with one another. And the reason for the collisions has to do with their position in the solar system. Asteroids are under the massive gravitational pull of the sun, of course, but they are also tugged at by the gravity of Jupiter and of Mars. This means their orbits aren't "even," like the orbits of Earth and bigger planets, but often get changed—they get tugged out of one orbital path and onto another. And thus they tend to smash into each other. It has been estimated that the average-size asteroid suffers a collision about once every hundred million years, which comes to quite a few collisions during billions of years. And naturally, as asteroids get broken into pieces by collisions, there are more and more pieces to collide with each other. The asteroid belt is literally a great rock-breaking machine in space!

And because of the ever-changing orbits of these little planetoids, many of them get tugged onto new paths, carrying them on collision courses with the inner worlds of the solar system. It is then that an event such as happened in Siberia in 1947 takes place.

The asteroid that entered Earth's atmosphere then was probably no more than 30 feet in diameter, about the size of a two-car garage. The instant it entered Earth's atmosphere, it began to rapidly heat up, glowing a dull red, a brighter red, then an intense yellow white. It was no longer an asteroid, it had now become what is called a bolide (a "fireball") or a meteor.

The reason for the intense heat is simply friction. Friction is the rubbing together of two things, and the faster they rub, the hotter they get. Rub your hands together rapidly for a few moments and see how warm they begin to feel. The asteroid had come into the atmosphere at a speed of probably from seven to twelve miles a second, and it and the air were rubbing against one another at that speed. The tremendous friction caused tremendous heat. Both the bolide and the air through which it was passing were burning. The bolide was glowing so brightly that, to the people who saw it, it seemed as bright as the sun. Portions of it were actually *melting* into a fine mist, leaving a trail of smoke, a long streak in the sky.

The heat and friction caused the bolide to break into fragments, but the fragments stayed loosely together. This cluster of rock and metal pieces approached the Siberian mountainside at a sharp angle, shearing off the tops of trees in its path the instant before it struck. When the pieces smashed into the mountainside, the explosion pushed the ground downward and outward, forming craters, and further shattering the fragments of bolide, bouncing them out of the craters to litter the mountainside. Now that the fragments had come to Earth, they were no longer called either asteroid or bolide. Now they had become what are called meteorites. The craters they made are called meteorite craters. The way these meteorite craters were formed is how many of the craters on the surface of the moon, Mars, Mercury, and the other inner planets were formed.

Because of Earth's protective atmosphere, which burns up the many small bits of rock and metal that come hurtling out of space every day, the planet is not at all as pocked and pitted as the moon or Mars. But it has its share of craters, for it has been struck by meteorites numerous times during its long life. Sometime between 15,000 and 40,000 years ago, a huge meteorite traveling at a speed of probably nine miles a second smashed into a rocky plain in what is now the state of Arizona and left a gigantic crater 4,150 feet wide and 570 feet deep. But this is far from being the largest meteorite crater on our planet. There are craters one and a half miles, two miles, and more than seven miles wide in Canada. And also in Canada, scientists have found a great *400-mile-wide* "dent" that may be the worn crater of an enormous meteorite that rocketed out of space and slammed into the earth many millions of years ago.

A great many actual meteorites and fragments of meteorites have been found on the ground. They consist of either iron sometimes mixed with other metals, stone, or a mixture of stone and metal. The largest meteorite ever found is a great egg-shaped, pitted lump of iron nearly 10 feet long and weighing 15½ tons. Most museums everywhere have at least one or two small meteorites, and if you ever get the chance to see one, don't miss it. You'll be looking at a genuine visitor from space— once perhaps circling far out between Mars and Jupiter!

Barringer Meteor Crater,
Winslow, Arizona

Comets—FLYING STARS

THE NIGHT SKY of Earth had changed. The familiar stars still glittered, the friendly moon still gleamed, but there was something else in the sky, an unfamiliar thing that had no business being there! It was a long, glowing shaft of light, bright at one end and fading into darkness at the other. It had appeared, suddenly, a few nights before and had seemingly grown brighter and nearer each night since.

"What can it mean?" whispered a woman, staring fearfully upward.

"They do say," muttered a man who stood beside her, "that it be an omen. A sign! They say it do foretell of great trouble to come upon the world! War! Or famine, or plague! Or even—" his voice sank, "the end of the world!"

Conversations such as this have probably taken place several times during many thousands of years—every time a comet has come near enough to be seen in the sky. A comet may take a number of different shapes. It may be a fuzzy, glowing ball some four or five times the size of the moon, like the comet that appeared in 1770. Or it may look like a large, brightly glowing star with a long, gleaming tail stretching across the whole horizon, like Halley's

Comet in 1910. But whatever its shape, a comet is an awesome and frightening sight when it suddenly appears in the sky, especially if you have no idea what it is. So, for thousands of years, people always regarded the coming of a comet as an omen of disaster.

Today, we know enough about comets not to be frightened of them—although, some people probably still would be. We know they're members of our solar system that travel in wide, elliptical orbits around the sun. We know why they seem to appear in the sky so suddenly, and we understand what makes them look as they do.

A comet comes toward the earth out of the farthest part of the solar system. Most comets can't be seen with a telescope until they're roughly between the orbits of Mars and Jupiter. Then, a comet may appear only as a tiny point of light with a faint haze around it. The tiny point of light, called the nucleus, is the center and "body" of the comet.

When the comet gets close enough to the sun, things begin to happen to it. The icy nucleus begins to melt, causing a hazy atmosphere to form around it. This hazy patch around the nucleus, called the coma,

swells up and brightens. And the comet may grow a tail, a faintly shining streamer trailing out behind it. But only if the comet is big enough, close enough to the sun, and close enough to Earth, can it be seen without a telescope. Actually, there are about three or four comets somewhere in the sky *every* night, but they are too small or too far away to be seen with ordinary eyesight.

The comet suddenly changes as it nears the sun because of the sun's heat and light. The nucleus of a comet does not shine with light of its own. It is a dark body, like a planet, and shines with reflected sunlight. The fuzzy coma around the nucleus is a cloud of gas, and as the nucleus warms up from the sun's heat, it releases more gas, so that the coma spreads out, becoming a ball of gas thousands of miles wide. The gas shines with reflected sunlight in much the same way a ground-glass reflector on a bicycle glows when a car's headlights hit it. This is what makes the head of the comet suddenly appear quite bright. It is the fuzzy halo of gas that gives a comet its name. The word *comet* comes from two Greek words meaning "hairy star."

A comet's tail, too, may also be made of gas, or it may be made up of dust given off by the nucleus. A dust type of tail reflects sunlight; a gas tail is fluorescent, or it glows. The tail streams out from the head of the comet because of a kind of pressure from the sun called photon pressure. (Photon pressure is light pressure. Particles of light strike particles of the comet's gas and dust, creating movement away from the sun.) As the comet is moving in its orbit toward the sun, this pressure pushes the gas or dust out behind the head of the comet. Similarly, as the comet's orbit carries it away from the sun, photon pressure pushes the gas or dust out in front of the comet's head.

The tail may take any number of different forms. It may be long and straight, resembling a flashlight beam. It may be a series of streamers or wavy patterns. It may look like a cloud or a string of knots. It may be curved, like the blade of a saber. The form of a comet's tail has mostly to do with its composition. A straight, bluish tail means it is made up of gas; a curved, yellowish tail means it is made up of dust. As for length, a comet tail can be as much as 100 million miles long!

Perhaps all this sounds as if we know comets inside out, but the fact is many features of the comet are still mysteries. For example, astronomers are not completely sure what the nucleus of a comet is made of. They think it is probably clusters of chunks of ice and frozen gas, mixed with tiny bits of rock and metal—like a snowball with sand mixed into it. As the coma nears the sun, the ice melts, releasing gas and dust, which enlarges the coma and forms the tail. The sandy-snowball nucleus of a comet may be from a fraction of a mile wide to as much as 10 miles wide.

There's also a mystery about where comets come from. Astronomers generally think that far out past Pluto, perhaps as far as halfway to the nearest star, there is a great "cloud" of comet material consisting of fragments of rock and frozen gas. The size of this cloud cannot be positively figured out, but astronomers think that if all the material in it were squeezed into a ball, the ball would be close in size to Earth.

Far away though it is, this cloud is held in place by the gravitational pull of the sun, and so it is part of the solar system. And yet, the material in the cloud is far enough away from the sun to be also affected by the gravity of other stars. The gravitational pull of other stars sometimes sends chunks of the cloud on new orbits—in toward the sun. The orbits of some of these comets carry them back out to the cloud after a time. Some apparently leave the solar system entirely, while others get grabbed by the gravity of giant Jupiter and become what astronomers call "short term" comets, which take up orbits that keep them well within the solar system until they finally break up and cease to exist as comets.

Over many thousands of years, a number of comets have passed near enough to Earth to be seen. But one comet in particular has become well known because it has made "return trips" every 76 to 79 years for more than 2,000 years. This is Halley's Comet, named after the astronomer who first realized that it was actually one comet on an orbit that kept bringing it back. It last visited us in 1910, and is due to show up again in 1986—so *you* might be able to see it!

As the nucleus of a comet heats up when it nears the sun, it leaves a trail of its smaller, solid particles behind it. Many of these tiny bits of rock and metal get pulled toward Earth by our planet's gravitational tug. When they enter our atmosphere, they become what we call meteors. Were you ever lucky enough to be looking up at the sky at night when a streak of light went flashing across it? "A shooting star," you probably said to yourself. That's what most people call them, but they're actually meteors. Most of them are comet bits, often no bigger than a grain of sand or a pinhead, that enter Earth's atmosphere and burn up from friction, causing a quick, flashing streak high in the sky. Scientists estimate that as many as 200 *million* meteors bright enough to be seen flash in Earth's night sky every 24 hours!

Several times a year, the earth's orbit takes it through a stream, or "swarm," of particles left behind by a comet, causing a meteor shower. Then, for a night or two, if the sky is clear and dark enough, a number of "shooting stars" can be seen.

A number of times during a century, the earth will pass through a very heavy swarm of comet particles. Then, if conditions are right, something spectacular happens. For a time, the night sky seems to be filled with darting sparks of light, as if all the stars in space were falling toward Earth!

Unfortunately, the meteor showers that result from the meetings with these heavy swarms can only be seen in certain places in the world, and sometimes, because of bad weather and other reasons, they can't be seen at all. But maybe you'll be lucky enough to be in the right place when one of these sky spectaculars occurs someday—and you'll see a "fireworks" display you'll never forget.

Stars—LIFE AND DEATH

WHEN YOU LOOK up at a single, twinkling star at night, you're not seeing what you think you are! For one thing, although the star you see looks frosty white, it is probably really a very different color. For another thing, what you think is *one* star may actually be two stars, or even more. And for a third thing, you're not even seeing the star as it is right now— you're seeing it as it was five years, or twenty years, or a hundred years, or even thousands of years ago!

A star is, like the sun, a huge ball of gas that is changing its mass—the gas it is made of—into energy, or heat and light. The heat and light go rushing off into space. But the stars are so far away from us, it takes the light from some of them hundreds, thousands, and even millions of years to reach us. And so the light you see as you look at a twinkling star may actually be light the star was giving off in 1492!

And the white light you see from a star does not reveal the star's true color. The star shining down upon our world, our sun, is yellow. Walking through a woods in the afternoon, you can see beams of yellow sunlight slanting through the trees. Where the rays fall upon a patch of grass or cluster of leaves, the patch takes on a golden tint. But imagine a world where the sun shines with a fierce white light. Everything would seem to glare, and there would be stark, black shadows. Imagine a world where everything, all day long, is faintly red-tinted, from the light of a red sun. Imagine a world with a blue sun. For stars may be any one of a number of different colors.

The color of a star depends upon how hot the star's surface is. When a piece of steel comes out of a steel mill furnace it glows white-hot. As it cools it turns yellowish, then orange, then red. So it is with stars. The fiercely hot star Rigel glows with an intense blue light, the hottest light of all. The star Sirius, which is about half as hot as Rigel, glows white. Procyon, a little less hot than Sirius, is bright yellow. Pollux, a little cooler still, glows orange, and Betelgeuse, a quite cool star, with a surface temperature of "only" about 5,500 degrees F., is red.

The heat, color, and brightness of a star depend on its size and mass. Bright blue stars such as Rigel are supergiant stars, with a mass many, many times greater than our sun. What astronomers call *main sequence* white stars have a somewhat greater mass than our sun has, while main sequence

48

red stars have less mass than that of our sun.

A main sequence star is simply an ordinary-size star that hasn't yet grown old. For when a star grows old, things happen to it that affect its size, color, and heat. When a main sequence star such as our sun grows old and begins to die, it swells up and becomes a giant. It has about the same amount of mass that it had when it was normal size, but that mass is now thinly spread out. So the giant is "cool"— a *red* giant. Aldebaran is such a red giant. Although it is about 25 times the diameter of our sun, its surface is about half as hot.

After a time, when the red giant has turned more of its mass into energy, it *collapses*. Gravity pulls it together, and it shrinks way, way down. It may become no bigger than Earth. However, it still has the great amount of mass it had before it collapsed, but now that mass is so tightly packed together that the tiny star is tremendously heavy. A piece of it no bigger than a pea would weigh about as much as a big truck! It becomes extremely hot at its surface and glows with a white brilliance— it has become a white dwarf star.

Most red stars are main sequence stars, smaller than our sun. And many white stars are main sequence stars, a bit bigger than our sun. But red giant stars and white dwarf stars are no longer main sequence stars. They aren't ordinary size, and they are old and dying. A white dwarf eventually burns out and becomes a dark hulk.

Every star dies sooner or later. But *when* a star dies depends upon how fast it is changing its mass into energy. A brightly glowing supergiant, perhaps 50,000 times as bright as our sun, turns out energy thousands of times as fast as the sun does, so it has a rather short life of about only ten million years or less. A small yellow star such as our sun has a nice long life expectancy of about ten billion years. After that, it will last a long time first as a red giant, then as a white dwarf. A little, cool, main sequence red star, changing its mass into energy at a far slower rate than our sun, lives for many of billions of years!

Not all stars die in the same way. Main sequence red stars slowly fade out and become dark cinders. Main sequence white, yellow, and orange stars puff up into red giants, collapse into white dwarfs, and burn out. Sometimes, a white dwarf that is very close to a larger star will flare up in a sudden explosion. From Earth, such an explosion looks like a bright new star suddenly appearing in the sky, and is called a *nova,* meaning "new." But, far from being a new star, a nova is just the dying "sputter" of a white dwarf. After a few days, or perhaps after months, the brightness fades, and the dwarf is less or no brighter than it was.

A supergiant blue star dies in a blaze of glory. Like a nova, it explodes—but its explosion is tremendous, a titanic blast that destroys the star and hurls a huge amount of the star's energy and mass out into space. This kind of explosion is called a supernova, and seen from Earth it is a light that may be billions of times brighter than the star's light was before the explosion.

A supergiant star explodes when its core suddenly collapses. Gravity pulls the core together so tightly, the star becomes smaller than a white dwarf—no more than about 10 miles wide—in a fraction of a second! Its surface explodes out in all directions.

The collapsed core of the supergiant star is packed together so tightly we can hardly imagine how dense it is. It is so heavy that a small handful of it would weigh millions of tons! About 200 such tiny, tight-packed stars have been found in various parts of space. They are sometimes called pulsars, because some seem to *pulse*—that is, they give off steady, even bursts of energy.

The huge, fiery mass of energy hurled into space by a supernova explosion becomes an enormous cloud of chemicals in the form of gas and dust. Such a cloud is called a *nebula,* which means "mist." There are a number of nebulas (or nebulae) in space. Most are simply clouds of dust and gas. Many of these are dark masses blotting out the stars behind them. Those with hot stars in them are bright.

In the year 1054, more than 900 years ago, Chinese astronomers suddenly saw what seemed to be a bright new star. What they were seeing, of course, was a supernova. Today, in the part of space where that supergiant blue star exploded, there is a great nebula, the Crab Nebula, so named because it looks a bit like a misty, many-legged crab. It is the cloud thrown off by the supernova. And in the center of the Crab there is a pulsar—the remains of a star seen to explode 900 years ago.

So, instead of being the birth of a new star, a supernova is the beginning of death for an old one. Yet, in a way, a supernova *is* also the beginning of a new star. For, astronomers have found that pressure waves from an exploding star's nebula, hitting clouds nearby, cause new stars to form! Gas in the clouds is slowly pulled together by gravity until it forms a collapsing ball that begins to glow as it turns its mass into energy—a new star! Several nebulas in our galaxy contain dark blobs that may be new stars being formed.

When new stars are born, it seems as if they are more likely to be born as twins than as an "only child." A star such as our sun, all by itself with no other star closer than about four light-years away, is not typical. Most stars are in pairs. Pairs of stars are called *binaries,* which means "two." It seems as though something about the way stars are formed makes them form in pairs. In fact, our sun *was* nearly one of a pair of stars. Had the planet Jupiter been just a bit bigger, with more mass, it would have become a star. Then the sun and Jupiter would have been a binary system.

And so you see, the glittering stars in our sky are like living things. They are born, they grow old, they die—and they give birth to new, young stars. In fact, stars are the very stuff of life itself. For scientists say our sun and its planets were formed out of the gas and dust thrown off by a dying star. And scientists also say life on our planet came from the matter of which the earth is formed. Thus every living thing on our world—plants, animals, and *you*—is made of matter that once glowed in the heart of a star, somewhere out in space, billions of years ago!

Mysteries—BLACK HOLES, QUASARS

A FEW THOUSAND light-years from our sun, in the group of stars known as Cygnus, there is a star called HDE 226868. It is a huge star, a supergiant, many times bigger than our sun, and very bright. And it is part of an awesome mystery.

Astronomers can tell that HDE 226868 is apparently a binary star—one member of a pair of stars so close together they revolve around each other. However, while HDE 226868 is big and bright, its companion star cannot be seen at all. It seems to be invisible!

There are a number of reasons why HDE 226868's companion might not be seen. For example, it might be much smaller, dimmer, and in a position where big HDE 226868 simply covers it up. However, astronomers have found that HDE 226868's companion is pulling gas away from the big star, and the gas is being turned into x-rays. Astronomers can tell where the x-rays are coming from, but they still can't *see* anything at that place. And that's the mystery—for it means HDE 226868's companion star may *truly* be invisible, and thus it isn't a star at all, but instead may be one of those mysterious, incredibly fantastic things astronomers call "black holes!"

And what is a black hole? Well, it is literally a hole in space—a hole with such a tremendous pull of gravity, nothing can get away from it, not even light. That's why it's invisible, and why it's called a *black hole.*

This may seem dreadfully hard to understand. Space is nothingness, and how can there be a hole in nothing? Furthermore, how can a hole have gravity?

Scientists explain it this way—when a very massive star begins to die, gravity pulls it into a much smaller ball. The larger the star, the smaller the ball it becomes, because the larger the star, the more gravity it has to pull it tighter together. A red giant, hundreds of times bigger than our sun, becomes a ball about the size of Earth. A much larger star, with a much greater amount of gravity, gets squeezed down into a tiny ball about 6 to 9 miles wide. Yet that tiny ball contains so much matter, squeezed together so tightly, it has a tremendous density and a tremendous surface gravity —a pull that's probably more than *10 billion times* greater than the gravity of an ordinary main sequence star. We know this to be a fact.

So, if an even bigger star, with an even

HALE TELESCOPE,
PALOMAR OBSERVATORY,
CALIFORNIA

greater mass and gravity, shrinks, many scientists think that in some cases it gets squeezed together so tightly it actually vanishes—it is squeezed out of existence! In other words, nothing is left of it *but* its gravity. It becomes a hole in space, a hole with such a tremendous pull of gravity that nothing, once pulled toward it, can get away from it, not even light! And many scientists think it's just such an invisible black hole that's gathering gases given off by HDE 226868.

Scientists have figured out that a black hole would have the shape of a ball, anywhere from about ten to several hundred miles wide. It would be surrounded by a disk of gas, dust, and particles it has pulled toward itself and that are falling into it. You can think of it as being somewhat like a whirlpool. Just as a whirlpool is a sort of swirling, funnel-shaped hole in water that whirls things down into itself, a black hole whirls and swirls gas, dust, particles of light, and other particles down into itself. Once these things enter it they can never come back out again.

But what becomes of the stuff that goes into a black hole? What happens to it and where does it go? Scientists are not at all sure. As to what happens to it, it may become pure energy, like sunlight. As to where it goes, it may somehow "travel" through the hole and come out in a very different part of space—and perhaps in a very different *time,* such as millions of years in the future! And some scientists think the matter may actually go into another universe—another space different from the one we are in! They wonder if black holes may be openings leading into different places in other spaces and other times!

If there really are such things as black holes—and some scientists are not sure black holes can exist—then there are sure to be millions of them in our galaxy alone! And if each black hole is slowly pulling matter into itself, there may come a time, perhaps in many trillions of years, when everything in our universe will have been pulled into a black hole!

There is another mystery in space—actually, several hundred mysteries of this same sort. In 1960, astronomers discovered an object that seemed to be a bright star giving off radio waves. Radio waves are a form of energy that can be picked up by a radio telescope either as bursts or a steady signal of sound. The object was bright enough to be a near star, but there was something about it that made astronomers sure it was *not* just an ordinary near star. For, it showed what astronomers call a "red shift."

All light forms a band called a spectrum that's like a rainbow, with colors running from blue to red. When an object in space is moving rapidly away from Earth, a portion of the light it gives off shows a movement, or *shift,* toward the red end of the spectrum. The larger the portion of light, the greater the red shift, and the greater the shift, the faster the object is moving, Many galaxies, moving away from our galaxy because of the expansion of the universe, show red shifts that tell us they are moving quite swiftly. And the starlike

radio telescope

54

thing the astronomers discovered showed a red shift that indicated it was moving away *very* fast. It couldn't be a near star.

The astronomers didn't know for sure what the thing was, but they called it a "quasi-stellar radio source," which simply means a starlike object giving off radio waves. That long name was quickly shortened to "quasar."

Since then, about 500 quasars have been discovered. They all seem to be moving away from us quite rapidly—some, almost as fast as the speed of light! And many seem to be more than a billion light-years away, which means they are the farthest objects that can be seen at the present time from Earth. They seem to be out at the very edge of the universe. Yet they are tremendously bright—because they are giving off about one hundred thousand billion times more energy than the sun!

What exactly are these quasars? There are a number of ideas about them. Many astronomers think quasars are actually galaxies—masses of millions of stars—that somehow give off enormous amounts of energy from somewhere in their centers. Other astronomers think quasars may really be much nearer, and perhaps smaller, than they seem to be. Perhaps they are objects that have been "thrown out" of our own galaxy at high speed, by some cause.

Still another idea, held by a few scientists, says quasars are nothing less than the *exits* of black holes; the tremendous amount of energy they are giving off is matter that was once pulled into the openings of black holes and converted into energy during its journey through the hole!

And some scientists simply think that the cause of quasars can't yet be understood, because our science just isn't yet far enough advanced to understand them. So, as you can see, quasars are certainly a mystery!

Black holes and quasars are probably the two biggest mysteries in space, but they aren't the only ones. About 1,100 light-years from Earth there is a strange, sharp-edged "red rectangle" that has astronomers puzzled. Nothing else in space is quite like it. Astronomers think it may be a new pair of binary stars forming, with a solar system around them! And, far off in the group of stars known as Cygnus, there is a mysterious, glowing, oval patch known as the "egg nebula." No one is at all sure what it may be.

All these mysteries are waiting to be solved. And other, perhaps even stranger mysteries are bound to be discovered in years to come. This is why the study of space, with its many mysteries that boggle the mind, is the most fascinating study in the universe!

60-inch reflecting telescope,
Mt. Wilson Observatory

Constellations—PATTERNS IN THE SKY

IF YOU LOOK up at the night sky at a certain time of year, you may see a fish, a goat, and a winged horse!

What you will *really* see, if the sky is clear enough, are stars. But if you look at all the stars for a little while, you will begin to notice that groups of them seem to form patterns. And long, long ago, many of these star patterns were given names such as "goat" and "fish."

You see, many thousands of years ago, prehistoric people paid a lot more attention to the stars than most people do today. Prehistoric hunters, shepherds, farmers, and sailors were often out all night beneath a great, clear sky blazing with stars, and they learned to watch the stars because the stars were useful to them. Before there were such things as compasses or maps, sailors and other people making long journeys could find their way by heading toward a certain star or stars. Before there were clocks, the rising of certain stars was used to mark off the hours of the night. And before there were calendars, the appearance of certain stars or groups of stars told of the start of a new season.

So, many of the people of long ago were quite familiar with the stars. And one of the things the first star watchers noticed right away was that groups of stars formed patterns that never changed. Because people used many of these star patterns, they gave them names. "Ah, the horse is rising tonight," one shepherd might say to another, as they watched their flocks. And his companion would know that he was speaking of a certain pattern of stars, the first sight of which meant that winter was coming on.

Today, we call these patterns of stars constellations, a word meaning something like "made of stars." And we still call many of the constellations by the name given them long ago. The names are in Latin, the language of ancient Rome, and you've probably heard many of them, such as *Taurus*, which means "bull," and *Leo*, meaning "lion." But although constellations are named for animals, birds, people, and such things as a harp, a clock, and a cup, most of them don't look a bit like the thing they are named after. You can't hope to see a group of stars that really has the shape of a bull, a lion, or a goat.

There are 88 constellations altogether, but it isn't possible to ever see them all at once. Certain constellations can only be

PHOENICIANS NAVIGATING
BY THE STARS

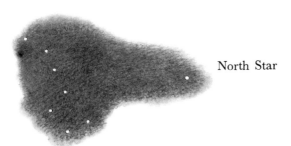

Big Dipper (Ursa Major)

North Star

ZODIAC
CONSTELLATIONS

Capricornus

Sagittarius

Scorpius

Libra

Virgo

Leo

Cancer

Gemini

Taurus

Aries

Pisces

Aquarius

seen from the northern half of the earth, and others can only be seen from the southern half. There are some constellations that can be seen best in the spring, and others are best viewed in summer, fall, or winter.

Even though the stars in a constellation may look as if they are close together, they are really far apart from one another. For example, in the constellation we call the Big Dipper, the star named Alkaid, at the very end of the dipper's handle, is about 210 light-years from Earth, while the star next to it in the handle, Mizar, is 88 light-years away. Thus, Alkaid and Mizar are about 122 light-years—more than 700 trillion miles—apart. They only seem to be near one another because of the way we see them from Earth, but from another part of space they wouldn't appear to be close together at all.

The reason why the stars in each constellation always stay together is also because of the way we see them from Earth. All the stars are moving, of course, and they are moving in many different directions. But they are all so tremendously far from Earth, it takes thousands of years for us to be able to see that they have moved. In a great many thousands of years, the stars will have moved enough so that all the constellations will look very different from the way they do now.

The constellations appear to move through the sky during the night. Each one, during its season, rises above the eastern horizon at a certain time, climbs up into the sky, then sinks back down westward, following a curved path. During its season,

each constellation rises a little higher each night until, one night, it reaches its highest point during the year. After that it will be a little lower each night, until finally all or most of it will be so far beneath the horizon it can no longer be seen—until its season comes around again.

Most constellations can only be seen in the evening sky during a particular season because the earth moves around the sun. As the earth makes this journey, it passes through parts of space from where the stars that form certain constellations can be seen, and those constellations then appear in our night sky. And as the earth continues to move, it passes out of that part of space, leaving those constellations behind until it returns to pass them again a year later.

However, even though the earth's Northern and Southern hemispheres look upon several different parts of space during our journey around the sun, the North and South poles always point toward the same part of space. And so, certain constellations in those parts of space can *always* be seen in the Northern and Southern hemispheres. The constellations called Ursa Major (Great Bear), Ursa Minor (Smaller Bear), Draco (Dragon), Cepheus (the name of a king in an ancient Greek myth), and Cassiopeia (Cepheus' queen), can be seen every night in the northern sky, although their positions change.

The one thing in the sky never to change position during the whole year, an object that hasn't changed its position for many centuries, is the star known as Polaris—the North Star. (Now, Polaris is slowly changing position, too, but it is taking many thousands of years.) The earth's North Pole points almost directly at Polaris, and because the poles are the only parts of the earth that don't change their position as the planet turns, the North Star is always almost straight above the North Pole. All the other stars seem to wheel around it in a great circle. For many centuries, sailors have used the North Star to find their way at sea. If they wanted to head north, they sailed toward the star; if they wanted to go south, they sailed away from it. To go west, they kept it on their right; and to go east, they sailed in the direction with the North Star to the left.

So the North Star has always been a very important star. Once you know where to look for it you can always find it, and if you don't know exactly where to look, one of the constellations in the northern sky will show you. The constellation called the Big Dipper is an easy constellation to see all year long. It forms part of the hindquarters of the Great Bear, and it looks like an old-fashioned water dipper seen from the side. The two stars that form the very front of the dipper's pan are brighter than the others and point toward the North Star. Just look along an imaginary line that runs from the star in the bottom of the pan through the one at the top, and the first big, bright star you'll see is the North Star. The North Star also happens to be at the very tip of the handle of the constellation called the Little Dipper or the Smaller Bear, Ursa Minor.

Constellations were important to astronomers of long ago, but astronomers of today do not pay much attention to them. They are useful only for dividing up the sky into sections so that astronomers can find things easily. For example, if an astronomer should see something odd in the cluster of stars called the Pleiades, and wants other astronomers to look there, they all know that the Pleiades are in the constellation Taurus, and can turn their telescopes right to the part of the sky where Taurus is to be found. But to *us* the patterns in the sky are still beautiful and, with just a little imagination, truly awe-inspiring!

Pronunciation Guide

Aldebaran	ahl-DEB-ah-rahn
Betelguese	BEH-tuhl-joohs
Callisto	kah-LIST-oh
Cassini	kah-SEE-nee
Cassiopeia	KAS-ee-yoh-PEE-yah
Cepheus	SEE-fee-yuhs
Ceres	SEER-eehs
Charon	CHAH-rohn
coma	KOH-mah
Cygnus	SIG-nuhs
Deimos	DY-mohs
Dione	dee-OHN
Draco	DRAY-koh
Enceladus	EN-seh-LAH-duhs
Europa	yuhr-OH-pah
Ganymede	GAN-ee-meed
Halley's (Comet)	HAY-leehs
Iapetus	ee-YAH-pah-TUHS
Io	I-yoh
Leda	Lee-dah
Mimas	MY-mahs
Miranda	muhr-AN-dah
nebula, nebulae	NEB-yoo-lah, NEB-yoo-lay
Nereid	NEER-ee-yuhd
nova	NOH-vah
nucleus	NOO-klee-yuhs
Olympus Mons	oh-LYM-puhs MOHNS
Phobos	FOH-bohs
Phoebe	FEE-bee
photon	FOH-tahn
Pleiades	PLY-ah-deehs
Polaris	poh-LAY-ruhs
Pollux	POH-luchs
Procyon	proh-SY-ahn
Proxima Centauri	PROKS-eh-mah sen -TAH-ree
Rhea	REE-yah
Rigel	RY-juhl
Schiaparelli	SHAP-ah-REL-ee
Sirius	SEE-ree-yuhs
Tethys	TETH-eehs
thermonuclear	THUR-moh-NOO-klee-YUHR
Uranus	YUHR-ahn-nuhs
Valles Marineris	VAL-uhs MAIR-uhn-AIR-uhs

Index

ALBUM OF ASTRONOMY

JUPITER'S STORMY BANDS of atmosphere, Saturn's icy-gleaming rings, the puzzling quasar whose existence perhaps tells us of the nature of the universe, the mysterious black hole whose discovery may *change* our ideas on the nature of space, and the distances—space so vast the human brain can just begin to think on it—this is the stuff of one science: astronomy.

The author and illustrator team of Tom McGowen and Rod Ruth is well known for a lively series of animal albums, from 1972's ALBUM OF DINOSAURS to the recent AL- BUM OF REPTILES. Astronomy presented a challenge for even this experienced pair. With data pouring in from NASA's space probes to Mars, Venus, and Jupiter, scientists' thoughts on what this news meant were constantly changing the face of the subject. Keeping up-to-the-minute was the subject's stiffest demand, and this book meets that demand.

Fourteen chapters reveal plenty of information on the basics of the universe, the sun, the planets, the lives of stars and comets, the mysteries of space, the patterns we see in the night sky. Over 60 black-and-white pictures help the reader visualize some of the tricky principles of space science, and each chapter opens with a wonderful full-color interpretation by artist Ruth of the latest facts about the surface of Venus or the formation of a star. An index and guide to pronunciation are included as essentials, and a look to the endsheets gives plans of both the northern and southern skies—maps of our neighbors in this galaxy and beyond. All in all, the ALBUM OF ASTRONOMY is an accurate and completely enjoyable treatment of one of today's most important sciences.

PRINTED IN U.S.A.

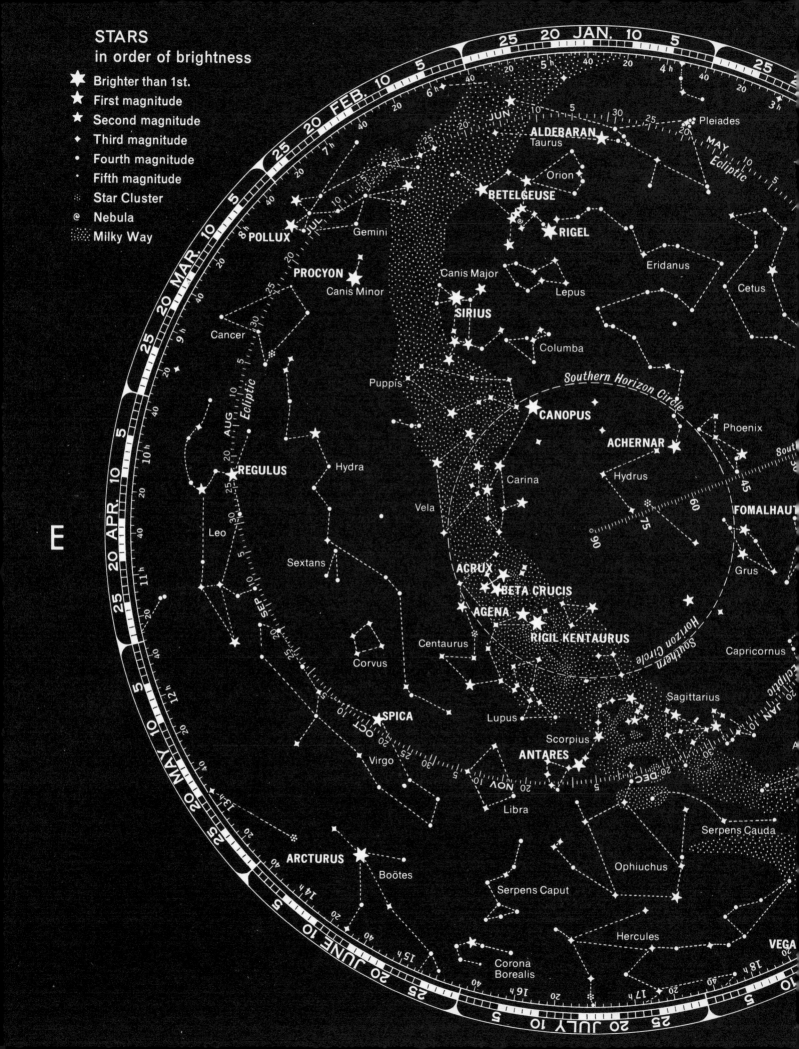